FabJob Guide to

Become a Bridal Salon Owner

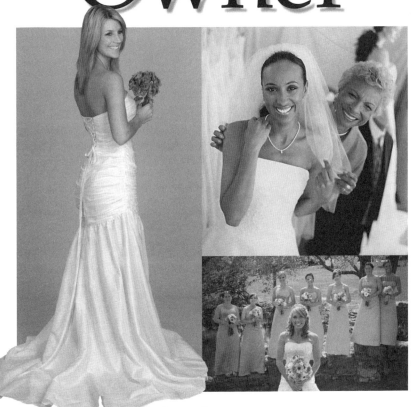

ALISA GORDANEER

FABJOB® GUIDE TO BECOME A BRIDAL SALON OWNER
by Alisa Gordaneer

ISBN: 978-1-897286-52-4

Library and Archives Canada Cataloguing in Publication

Gordaneer, Alisa
FabJob guide to become a bridal salon owner / Alisa Gordaneer.

Also available in electronic format.
Contributing author: Pamela Skillings.
ISBN 978-1-897286-52-4

1. Bridal shops--Management. 2. New business enterprises.
I. Skillings, Pamela II. FabJob III. Title. IV. Title: Become a bridal salon owner.

HD9941.3.A2G67 2009   381'.4568716   C2009-905102-8

Important Disclaimer: Although every effort has been made to ensure this guide is free from errors, this publication is sold with the understanding that the authors, editors, and publisher are not responsible for the results of any action taken on the basis of information in this work, nor for any errors or omissions. The publishers, and the authors and editors, expressly disclaim all and any liability to any person, whether a purchaser of this publication or not, in respect of anything and of the consequences of anything done or omitted to be done by any such person in reliance, whether whole or partial, upon the whole or any part of the contents of this publication. If expert advice is required, services of a competent professional person should be sought.

About the Websites Mentioned in this Guide: Although we aim to provide the information you need within the guide, we have also included a number of websites because readers have told us they appreciate knowing about sources of additional information. (**TIP:** Don't include a period at the end of a web address when you type it into your browser.) Due to the constant development of the Internet, websites can change. Any websites mentioned in this guide are included for the convenience of readers only. We are not responsible for the content of any sites except FabJob.com.

FabJob Inc.
19 Horizon View Court
Calgary, Alberta, Canada T3Z 3M5

FabJob Inc.
4616 25th Avenue NE, #224
Seattle, Washington, USA 98105

To order books in bulk, phone 403-949-2039
To arrange a media interview, phone 403-949-4980

www.FabJob.com
THE DREAM CAREER EXPERTS

Contents

About the Authors

Lead author **Alisa Gordaneer** has worked for many years as a writer and editor, focusing on lifestyle, business and more. She has also spent many years working in retail, where she's had a front-row seat for countless brides' wedding preparations through her work at her family flower shop. You can read about her own wedding dress in the collection *My Wedding Dress: True-Life Tales of Lace, Laughter, Tears and Tulle* (Knopf Canada, 2007). Alisa is also the author of several other FabJob guides including the *FabJob Guide to Become a Florist* and the *FabJob Guide to Become a Craft Store Owner*.

Contributing author **Pamela Skillings** is an entrepreneurship expert and career coach based in New York City. Through her company, Skillful Communications, Pamela provides business coaching and consulting services to both large and small companies, including boutiques and apparel designers. Pamela is also the author of the entrepreneurship guide *Escape from Corporate America: A Practical Guide to Creating the Career of Your Dreams* (Ballantine, 2008) and a contributing writer and editor for About.com, part of the New York Times Company. Previously, Pamela worked as a senior marketing and training executive with Fortune 500 companies including Citigroup and MasterCard International. Pamela's material on opening a bridal boutique was previously published in the *FabJob Guide to Become a Boutique Owner*.

Acknowledgements

Thank you to the following experts (listed alphabetically) for generously sharing bridal salon insider information, and business and marketing advice in this FabJob guide. Opinions expressed in this guide are those of the author or editors and not necessarily those of experts interviewed for this guide.

- *Elizabeth Andrei*
  Here Comes the Bridesmaid,
  New York, NY
  www.bridesmaids.com

- *Karen Caprio*
  Owner/designer, Bellina Bridal,
  New York, NY
  **www.etsy.com/shop.php?
  user_id=6178674**

- *Keri Chantler and Jenni Hailer*
  Owners, Twirl Boutique,
  Scottsdale AZ
  www.twirlboutique.com

- *Ernie Comer*
  Founder, Dressprice.com
  www.dressprice.com

- *Eva D'Avella*
  Owner, A Fairytale Wedding,
  Los Angeles, CA
  www.afairytalewedding.com

- *Daniela Isabella FerdicoFaget*
  Owner, Bella Signature Design Inc.,
  Seattle, WA
  www.bellasignature.com

- *Lillie Garrido*
  Owner, Soiree Productions Wedding
  Studio, White Couture Designer
  Bridal and Tuxedos, Park City, UT
  www.soireeproductions.com

- *Sidney Green*
  Vice-president, software sales,
  BBL Systems

- *Keri Herndon-Brown*
  Owner, Events By Keri,
  Atlanta, GA
  www.eventsbykeri.com

- *Haley Hughes*
  Owner, En Vogue Events,
  Houston, TX
  www.envogueevents.com

- *Richard Markel*
  President, Association of Wedding
  Professionals International
  www.afwpi.com

- *Shane McMurray*
  The Wedding Report
  www.theweddingreport.com

- *Tanya W. Porter*
  Author, *Wedding Planning Guide,
  A Bride's Workbook* and *The Art of
  Wedding Coordination*, and owner
  Weddings, Etc. LLC,
  Englewood, CO
  www.weddingsbytanya.com

- *Susan Alexander Shapiro*
  Founder, BravoBride,
  Seattle, WA
  www.bravobride.com

1. Introduction

"The bridal business is THE business to go into. Our daily job is to help create the perfect look for our customers' dream wedding. What could be more fun? Furthermore, whether the economy is up or down, thousands of weddings take place every year."

— Keri Chantler and Jenni Hailer, owners,
Twirl Boutique, Scottsdale AZ

Congratulations on saying "I Do" to your dream of becoming a bridal salon owner. You're taking the first step toward a career that will let you experience all the joy of a perfect wedding day, over and over again. You're about to be surrounded by beautiful gowns made from gorgeous, luxurious fabrics. You'll get to sell lovely shoes, exquisite accessories and even sparkling, exotic jewelry. You'll feel like a fairy godmother every time you help an excited client into her perfect wedding dress. Every day, you'll have the satisfaction of knowing you've helped to make someone's most cherished dreams come true.

People who choose to run bridal salons tend to have a lot in common with each other, and you're probably already more like seasoned bridal industry professionals than you think. You've probably got a romantic streak, as well as a sense of beauty that draws you to the finer things in life. You may find yourself drawn to fashion magazines and boutiques where you can see the latest and most beautiful couture outfits.

You've probably already got a good sense of style, and have an eye for what looks best on just about anyone. Or maybe you've helped a friend or family member choose her own wedding gown and fell in love with the whole glamorous world of weddings. In any case, you're in the right place, because your love of beauty, fashion and the glamour of weddings will help you achieve success as a bridal salon owner.

Chances are, you might have already worked in retail, and perhaps even in fashion retailing. If so, you'll find that nothing compares to the satisfaction of running your own store and seeing first-hand the rewards that come with all the hard work you put in.

This chapter sets you out on your path towards becoming a bridal salon owner. We will discuss aspects of the wedding industry and briefly touch on the different types of bridal salon niches you can choose (we'll explore possible niches in more depth in section 3.1). We'll also discuss the benefits of this exciting career and outline the steps you'll need to take in order to get started.

1.1 A Growth Industry

No matter what the current economic climate, women will always get married. The wedding industry in the United States alone is currently estimated as being worth approximately $86 billion a year, according to the Association for Wedding Professionals International. This includes everything from wedding gowns to caterers to photographers and entertainment, but the market for bridal wear represents a significant portion of the total.

According to The Wedding Report, American brides in 2008 spent an average of $1,266 on their gowns, and a combined total of more than $600 on their veil or headpiece and accessories. In 2007, the most recent year for which U.S. Census demographic information is available, there were more than 2.2 million weddings in the United States alone. This means that total spending on brides' outfits alone could be estimated at more than $4 billion in one year. Add in bridesmaids' dresses, tuxedos rentals and other bridal wear accessories and you have a booming industry.

A significant factor in the North American bridal wear market sector is the fact that the median age of those getting married for the first time has increased over the past 30 years. For example, in Canada in the 1970s, the median age of first marriage was 25 years old for men and 22 years old for women. In 2003, the median age of first marriage had increased to age 30 for men and 28 for women. The trend toward later age of first marriage is similar in the U.S., although not as dramatic. In the U.S. in the early 1970s, the numbers were 23 years for men and 21 for women. By 2003, the median age of first marriage had risen to 27 for men and 25 for women.

The rising age of first marriage across North America suggests that men and women are waiting until their jobs and careers are established, when they possibly have more financial resources to spend on the weddings of their dreams. This is supported by the fact that average spending on weddings has increased during the same period.

Another growing sector in the wedding is that more countries, including Canada and some U.S. states, are beginning to recognize same-sex unions. As a result, the market for wedding wear has started to grow even further. According to Statistics Canada, 42% of same-sex couples who married in 2003 in British Columbia (the only province that kept track of marriages by the gender of marrying couples) were female, which could indicate a new niche in the bridal wear market.

A few other encouraging trends in wedding spending have been reported by The Wedding Report as recently as October, 2008. The first is that, while they are willing to cut costs by inviting fewer guests and reigning in their wedding budgets in other areas, women are not willing to spend less on their wedding dresses. Brides are also more frequently opting for more expensive dresses. Further, because more brides now come from multicultural backgrounds than ever before, they are purchasing more than one dress for their weddings because they are undertaking more than one ceremony. All of this suggests that the bridal salon market will continue to flourish through the coming years.

1.2 Owning a Bridal Salon

As a bridal salon owner, you'll be helping brides put together the outfit of their dreams for their big day. To do this, you'll stock a selection of products that they can buy to wear for their wedding celebrations. You'll also offer a range of services that helps ensure those products fit perfectly, are exactly the right color, and are even worn in just the right way.

1.2.1 Products

A bridal salon sells apparel and accessories for members of a wedding party to wear and use before, during and after their wedding ceremony. It may also sell formalwear for other occasions, such as proms, graduations, fancy events and cocktail parties. Here are just some of the products you might choose to carry in your bridal salon.

Wedding Gowns

This is the mainstay of your business—the dresses of a bride's dreams. Bridal salons sell a range of gowns, from custom and couture gowns that are made specifically for a bride, to ready-to-wear and off-the-rack dresses that are available right away. These dresses may be designed by an outside designer or couture house or they may be designed by the salon's in-house designer. A wedding gown is often the biggest single clothing purchase a woman will ever make. Some salons now also offer modest gowns for brides being married in religious ceremonies, as well as gowns meant to reflect different cultural traditions.

Bridesmaid Dresses and Formal Gowns

Gowns, cocktail dresses and party dresses are all being worn by a bride's attendants these days, so most bridal salons stock a wide range of styles and colors to help co-ordinate a wedding party's overall look. These gowns are typically less elaborate than a bride's gown. In addition to wedding parties, these dresses may be purchased by customers for proms and other events.

A bridal salon also sells gowns to be worn by mothers of the marrying couple, and dresses to be worn by children in the wedding party, including junior bridesmaids and flower girls.

Men's Formal Wear

A bridal salon may stock a selection of tuxedos and formal suits to be worn by the men in the wedding party, along with accessories such as waistcoats, cummerbunds and pocket squares or handkerchiefs that co-ordinate with the wedding party's outfits. These items may be rented or purchased outright. Renting of men's formal wear is also suitable for proms and other formal occasions when renting is preferable to purchasing such a suit.

Shoes

Some salons stock wedding shoes in a variety of styles and colors to co-ordinate with the gowns they sell. As an added service, many offer custom dyeing services to co-ordinate shoes purchased elsewhere with dress colors.

Lingerie

From the classic garter to brassieres, bustiers, corsets, girdles, slips and hosiery worn beneath a wedding dress to ensure its flattering shape, to elegant or saucy nightwear meant to be worn on the wedding night, many salons carry lingerie items as additional sales items.

Accessories

Many brides want an elegant veil or sparkly tiara to accent their wedding dress, but there are many more accessories made just for weddings. These include gloves and wraps for elegance or warmth, fancy umbrellas for sun or rain protection, hair accessories such as jeweled clips and barrettes, jewelry such as earrings, or necklaces and brooches to complement a bridal look. Other accessories include secondary items like pillows for the ring bearer to carry the rings on, guest books and pens, decorated cake knives, and even purses and tote bags for the wedding party to use on the big day.

To-Be-Wed Gear

Many brides now choose to outfit their bridal party for the events leading up to the ceremony, including the bridal shower, the rehearsal dinner and the bride's "bachelorette" party. Many of these events are more casual than the wedding itself, and so there is now a range of casual wear to stock, including embellished t-shirts, hoodies, tank tops, baseball hats and underwear. These are often printed with funny sayings like "Bride-to-Be" or "The Future Mrs. Smith."

1.2.2   Services

A bridal salon owner may choose to offer a number of services to clients. Some of these services, such as fittings, are more crucial than others. Most bridal salons offer measuring and fitting services, but more complicated services, such as custom-designed gowns, can be offered if you choose. Here are some services that your bridal salon may offer.

Measuring

Making notes of a client's measurements ensures that their gown will fit perfectly. A bridal salon employee will measure the client's body with a measuring tape to gather information about the length of their body from the hollow of the neck to floor, their bust, waist and hips, and their arms from shoulder to wrist.

Fittings

When a dress arrives, or sometimes as it is being sewn if it is a custom dress, a client must try it on to make sure it fits correctly. These fittings are held at the bridal salon, and require a staff member to oversee the process to ensure the dress fits well. The staff member will also make note of any changes needed.

Custom Design

If you or a staff member is a keen fashion designer, you may choose to offer custom-designed wedding gowns based on clients' descriptions and desires. This is a premium service, as each gown must be designed, sewn and fitted well in advance, and requires numerous hours of work time. To offer this service, you will need to ensure you have sufficient staff, materials and time in order to deliver this service in a timely manner, while still maintaining your store's regular operations.

Custom Alterations

If you employ a seamstress on your staff, you may offer custom alterations in-house. This service ensures you are able to pay particular attention to a client's needs, and to change a dress to meet her wishes or size. However, if you are not able to offer this service yourself, you may offer referrals to skilled seamstresses in your area, who can help ensure each gown fits perfectly.

Personal Shopping

A personal shopping service helps brides find options for outfits for themselves or their wedding party. The personal shopper searches wholesalers' and designers' catalogues to find the types of outfits a bride has in mind, and makes suggestions to her. They may also do the same for accessories and other items.

Hair and Makeup

Some salons offer hair and makeup services for brides on their wedding day. If you do not have the ability or resources to provide these, you could offer a referral service to trusted hairdressers and makeup artists in your area.

Wedding Dressers

A wedding dresser attends to the bridal party in they place they are dressing for their event and helps the bride and attendants into their outfits. This is particularly important if there are elaborate outfits or if there are many members of the wedding party who will need to be dressed in a short amount of time. Having a dresser who knows how the outfits are meant to be worn, and who can be on hand for last-minute styling, is an invaluable service to many brides.

Wedding Gown Cleaning and Preservation

After the wedding, many brides choose to have their gown preserved in an archival-quality case that will let them keep their dress as pristine as their memories. While the actual cleaning service is typically provided by a drycleaner, some salons offer this service as well. If you don't have the facilities to clean and preserve a dress, you could arrange with a local drycleaner to provide this service to your customers.

Rentals

Some salons offer rental apparel, including wedding gowns, formal-wear and tuxedos. Whether or not you offer this service depends on your clientele. If you are located in an area where short engagements or "quickie" weddings are the norm, it may make sense to offer rentals to accommodate bridal parties who simply need something to wear, and soon.

Service Coordination

Because many wedding parties now live great distances away from each other, some salons offer coordination services to make sure that attendants' outfits are coordinated, fittings are scheduled in a timely way, and even let family members weigh in on a bride's choice of dress. Using the Internet and computer scheduling software, salons are able to help keep an entire wedding party's outfits organized and on time.

1.3   Benefits of Being a Bridal Salon Owner

Having your own bridal boutique is exciting enough, but being a bridal salon owner is about more than just having your own shop. It comes with a number of other built-in benefits, too.

Sharing Other People's Happiness

Being a bridal salon owner lets you have a window into people's lives at one of their happiest moments. You'll feel good about helping brides find the perfect dress, and helping attendants look their best. The results of your work will be displayed in treasured photographs and held in customers' dearest memories for years to come. "Most of your customers are happy!" observes Haley Hughes, of En Vogue Events in Houston. "You get to deal with clients who are planning an event together to celebrate their love, and you get to be a part of it." As Lillie Garrido, owner of White Couture Designer Bridal and Tuxedos in Park City, Utah, says, "Weddings are a happy occasion and working with brides and their families is rewarding because of it. You're helping to make their day."

A Fashionable Business

As a bridal salon owner, you'll have the opportunity to see and buy the latest fashions in wedding wear from around the world. You'll read fashion magazines to look for the latest trends in wedding couture, and watch fashion television to keep up on fashion news. As Susan Alexander Shapiro, founder of BravoBride, puts it, "It's rewarding to help brides find items that make their big day perfect. Every year styles change and every bride is different, so it is definitely never boring!"

Travel

To find inventory for your salon, you'll have the opportunity to travel to fashion shows, bridal expos and trade shows around the country and overseas. Combining work with pleasure you'll visit exciting locations to gather beautiful fabrics and inventory. And best of all, you'll be able to write off these trips as a business expense.

Community Connections

Being a bridal salon owner offers you a chance to connect with your local community and its most important celebrations. Not only will you get to know members of local society, but you'll get to be part of prom season, graduations and holiday events as customers turn to you for all their formalwear needs.

If you go out to a lot of events, or have lots of parties, you'll always have something fabulous to wear. You'll have an inventory of hundreds of cocktail gowns, party dresses and formalwear to choose from. And what better advertising than to say the gorgeous dress you're wearing came from your own shop?

Beautiful Surroundings

Your inventory of gorgeous gowns, fabrics, accessories and more will let you be surrounded by beautiful things all day long. You'll have lovely textures to feel, sights to see and even perfumes to smell. You'll work with your hands to create beautiful ensembles, and use your sense of style and fashion to help every customer become a beautiful bride.

Financial Rewards

Even if you aren't in it for the money, it's hard to ignore the fact that there's a lot of money to be made in the bridal salon industry. A wedding dress is typically the most expensive single clothing purchase a woman makes in her life. According to The Wedding Report, in 2008 brides in the United states spent, on average, $1,300 on their dress alone. In addition, they spent an average of $301 on a veil, and $321 on accessories to go with their wedding outfit.

These are just averages, though. A custom-designed or couture wedding dress can cost as much as $10,000 or more. Average spending on weddings is in the range of $20,000 to $30,000 per wedding, but some brides today choose to spend much more. By providing the products brides want and helping to make their big day as special as possible, you could find yourself earning an income that's limited only by your energy and salon capacity.

1.4 Inside This Guide

The FabJob Guide to Become a Bridal Salon Owner is organized to help take you step-by-step through the basics you will need to open and operate your own salon. The chapters are organized as follows:

Chapter 2 (*"Developing Your Skills"*) explains how to learn the skills you will need as a bridal salon owner. It covers ways of learning from experts and through observation. You will also discover how to "earn while you learn" by getting a job in the retail clothing industry or in another business related to the wedding industry. You'll also find resources for learning more, both through formal fashion industry training programs and through self-study options.

Chapter 3 (*"Starting Your Bridal Salon"*) will help you decide what kind of salon you should open. This chapter discusses different niches you can fill, from couture to resale bridal salons. It will also help you decide whether to buy an existing store or open a new store. It also explains what you need to get started, including your business plan, start-up financing, store name, and other important matters.

Chapter 4 (*"Setting Up Your Store"*) offers the information you need to actually set up your store. It gives advice on how to choose a location, get merchandise to sell, and arrange displays. You will also discover what equipment and supplies you will need.

Chapter 5 (*"Store Operations"*) takes you into the day-to-day challenge of running your store once it's open. It explains how to develop a procedures manual, and covers inventory management, financial management and pricing.

Chapter 6 (*"Marketing Your Business"*) shows you ways to bring customers into your store through advertising, promotional opportunities, and special events like Bridal Expos and trunk sales. You'll also learn about customer service, particularly as it relates to brides.

By following the steps in this guide, you will be well on your way to living your dream — opening your own successful bridal salon, and helping your joyful clients find the wedding gowns of their dreams.

2. Getting Ready

This chapter explains the kinds of skills you'll need to succeed as a bridal salon owner, and offers advice on how to develop those skills informally (learning on your own) and through more formal routes (courses, diplomas, certificates, and so on, at educational institutions). You don't necessarily need to go to school to learn this job, but there are a few courses and programs you might want to investigate if it would help you build a particular skill.

2.1 Skills and Knowledge You Will Need

Chances are good that you already have many of the skills, and much of the knowledge, you'll need to become a successful bridal salon owner. The key is to identify your areas of strength, which will give you additional confidence as you go into this business, and to fill in any gaps in your experience or knowledge in order to have as successful a start as possible.

The following self-evaluation quiz will help you figure out where you might need to build your skills, and where your own experience and personality will already help you along.

2.1.1   Self-Evaluation Quiz

Self-Evaluation Quiz

Below are some questions that reflect traits shared by many bridal salon owners. Make a mental note or put a checkmark next to all that are a "yes" for you.

- ❑ Do people consider you to be a good listener?

- ❑ Do you communicate ideas clearly when talking?

- ❑ Do you understand body language?

- ❑ Do your friends often turn to you for fashion suggestions or clothing advice?

- ❑ Are you good at working with your hands to create beautiful things?

- ❑ Do you love shopping for just the right outfit or the most gorgeous dress?

- ❑ Do you love predicting the kinds of outfits that will be hot next season?

- ❑ Are you often designing or making outfits and dresses for yourself or friends?

- ❑ Are you passionate about quality fabrics, accessories and materials?

- ❑ Are you crazy about accessorizing and finding the perfect accessory pieces and shoes to go with each outfit?

❏   Are you constantly buying fashion magazines and watching fashion television?

❏   Are you good at coordinating the needs of a group of people so everyone ends up happy?

These 12 questions offer insight into characteristics typical of individuals who enter and succeed in the bridal salon business. How did you do? If you answered "yes" to all of these questions, you already have qualities found in successful bridal salon owners. Even if you answered "no" to some, you can still be successful. Keep in mind that the skills and knowledge you need to succeed as a bridal salon owner can be learned. So let's take a look at the specific skills and knowledge that can help you succeed in your own bridal salon. Later in this chapter you'll find plenty of resources to develop these skills through education and self-study.

2.1.2   Interpersonal Skills

Having effective interpersonal skills is handy for many industries, but it's particularly important for bridal salon owners. You're dealing with brides, family members, and wedding parties who may live in different parts of the world, and have different ideas about what their needs are. Helping each person feel special, while accomplishing a unified whole, takes understanding and effective communication.

This section offers some tips to enhance the interpersonal skills that can help you have excellent relationships with your customers as well as your employees, suppliers, landlord, banker, and everyone else you do business with. Other parts of this book offer advice for dealing with specific situations that may arise in your business.

Listening

While listening seems like an easy skill to master, most of us experience challenges in at least one of the following areas involved in listening: paying attention, understanding, and remembering. You can become a better listener by focusing fully on someone when they are speaking. Here are some ways to do that:

- Don't interrupt the other person. Hear them out.

- Keep listening to the other person, even if you think you know what they will say next. If you make assumptions, you may miss the point they're making.

- Ask questions in order to clarify what the other person has said. Take notes if necessary.

- Don't be distracted by outside interference. Loud noises, the other person mispronouncing a word, or even an uncomfortable room temperature can break your concentration and distract you from the conversation.

- Give feedback to the other person. Nod occasionally; say things like "I see," and smile, if appropriate. Let them know you're listening.

- Use paraphrasing. In other words, repeat back in your own words your understanding of what the other person has said. It can help alleviate misunderstandings later on.

Verbal Skills

Clear communication is essential because you will need to explain your store's sales or return policy, and you will need to describe to customers your current inventory. When making sales, customers can become frustrated if they find it difficult to understand what you're saying. To improve your verbal communication skills, ask friends or a vocal coach for feedback on any areas that could be improved, such as: use of slang, proper grammar, or altering your tone of voice to eliminate any harshness. (You can find vocal coaches in the Yellow Pages or online.)

Reading Non-Verbal Messages

In addition to hearing what people say, a skilled business owner also notices non-verbal communication (tone of voice, facial expression, body language, etc.). These signals can give you valuable clues about what the other person is thinking.

For example, did a customer fold their arms when you made a particular suggestion? If so, they may be communicating that they disagree, even if they don't actually say so. Although body language can't tell you precisely what someone is thinking, it can give you clues so you can ask follow-up questions, even as basic as "How do you feel about that?" If you want to improve this skill, you can find some excellent advice in the book *Reading People*, by Jo-Ellan Dimitrius and Wendy Mazzarella.

2.1.3   Business Skills

If you are well prepared for being a business owner, the better the chances are that your bridal salon will be a success. It's crucial to know where your business stands financially at all times. While you don't have to learn it all, staying on top of your accounting will help you avoid finding yourself in the awful position of being out of cash to pay your bills or replenish your inventory.

Running a successful bridal salon requires an overlap of a variety of business skills. Aside from a knowledge and expertise about the particular products you sell (and training employees to be knowledgeable as well), you will need to know about:

- Business planning

- Financial management

- Merchandising

- Operations management

- Inventory management

- Hiring and supervising employees

- Marketing and sales

The more you can keep your expenses down while building a solid customer base to build sales volume, while at the same time turning over inventory frequently, the more successful you will be. For some of these tasks, you can hire employees or contractors to help you, such as a bookkeeper or someone who can handle the marketing and promotion for your business. Keep in mind, though, that the fewer people you need to hire to help you manage your business, the lower your overall costs of running the business. An investment in a few courses to develop these skills can pay for itself very quickly.

Developing business skills takes time, so be thorough, and don't be in such a rush that you neglect to fill in any gaps in your knowledge or skills. Experience you have in other retail environments can be helpful, and there are a number of ways you can develop your skills and knowledge in all of these areas. In this chapter, you'll find specific ideas to help you increase your experience and knowledge of running a bridal salon. You'll also find detailed advice throughout the remaining sections of this guide.

You will probably find reading the entire guide before you launch your business helpful, but you can quickly identify particular areas you may want to focus on by reviewing the table of contents. For example, section 5.5 provides advice on financial management, covering everything from budgeting to bookkeeping to building wealth, and section 3.5 gives you advice about start-up financial planning. Both these sections provide website links to online resources to help you find further help in these areas.

One tool for helping you to focus on what business skills are involved in being a business owner is business planning. Section 3.4 looks in detail at how to develop a business plan to get your business up and running by outlining and clarifying what products you will offer, deciding how you will finance your business, creating a market plan, etc. In addition to addressing these important business issues, a business plan will also help you to understand some of the other basic "hard" skills required of a business owner, such as marketing and accounting skills.

The Canada Business website at **www.canadabusiness.ca** has a great deal of helpful information for anyone thinking of starting their own business. They offer the following tips to new entrepreneurs for identifying and creating a unique service:

- Take advantage of a market switch

- Capitalize on a growth trend

- Take advantage of new fads

- Cover market gaps or shortages

- Imitate a successful product or idea

- Transfer a concept from one industry to another

- Invent a new product or service

- Create a market demand

- Serve unique customer groups

- Take advantage of circumstances

- Find people with under-used skills

Other Business Skills

In addition the business skills listed above, you will need to deal with a good amount of paperwork. This includes handling important business and legal issues pertaining to your business such as collecting and paying sales taxes, obtaining proper licenses to operate your business, and maintaining adequate insurance for your business. We'll discuss some of these issues in greater detail later on, but it's important to note that you will want to educate yourself on these issues and develop these skills if you do not already have them before you open your business.

Research Skills

Having good research skills is another important asset. You will need to use these skills from the moment you begin developing your business plan (including the population demographics of any areas in which you are considering opening your bridal salon), searching for the right location for your business, finding vendors and suppliers, learning about new trends and products, and other purposes.

Computer Skills

You will also need to know how to operate computers and software and use the Internet, as these are key for tracking sales data, inventory, and other important information. Computer skills can be learned, and many local school districts, community and other colleges offer continuing education or extension courses on how to operate a PC or Mac, as well as how to use several major software programs and making use of the Internet for research and marketing.

Resources for Developing Business Skills

The following resources can help you develop your business skills:

SBA

The Small Business Administration (SBA) is a leading U.S. government resource for information about licensing, taxes, and starting a small business. You can find a range of resources including information on financing your new business, business plans and much more at **www. sba.gov**.

SCORE

The Service Corps of Retired Executives (SCORE) is an organization of U.S. volunteers who donate their time and expertise to new business owners. You can find information on taxes, tips for starting your business, or even find a mentor who will coach you and help you maximize your chances of succeeding as a new business owner. Visit them at **www.score.org**.

Canada Business

This Canadian government website offers information on legislation, taxes, incorporation, and other issues of interest to Canadian business owners or those who do business in Canada. For more information and a list of services they offer visit their website at **www.canadabusiness.ca**.

2.1.4   Bridal Salon Skills and Knowledge

Manual Dexterity

As a bridal salon owner, you may be working with your hands to help brides try on dresses, create beautiful veils, and even to sew or embellish wedding gowns. Unless you have someone else on staff to handle these tasks, it's important to be able to hold small items like needles and beads, and to gather fabrics by hand. Any crafting skill you might have will come in handy here. Consider any experience you've had in needlework, fabric arts and sewing to be a valuable asset.

Fabric and Product Knowledge

You'll need inventory for your salon, and your skills at shopping (which include comparing fabrics, outfits and accessories, and choosing the best products at the best prices) will be essential to your success. If you spend a lot of time in fabric stores or poring over fashion magazines, you're probably already familiar with many of the fabric, pattern and design options available to bridal salon customers. Your knowledge of this field will help you advise your customers on the best choices to go with their ideal vision and ideal budget.

Predicting Trends

Are you the one in your circle who's always wearing the latest fashions a season sooner than everyone else? You probably spend a lot of time reading fashion magazines and blogs, and find yourself thinking ahead to the kinds of items that will be popular next. Your ability to predict what will be popular in a few months or even a year will help your high-fashion clients choose dresses that are truly on the cutting edge.

Coordinating Needs

While the ability to coordinate and meet the specific needs of a group of people is a handy skill for many industries, it's particularly important for bridal salon owners. Helping each person feel special while accomplishing a unified whole requires the skills of co-ordination, diplomacy and understanding. This will involve a high degree of organizational ability to help you keep track of customer orders, fitting schedules, who's who in each wedding party, etc.

2.2   Learning by Doing

2.2.1   Work in a Retail Clothing Store

Several of the store owners we spoke with said they had originally worked for another store. This can be a valuable way to learn much-needed skills for running your own bridal salon one day. Not only will you learn how to deal with customers, you will more than likely learn how to use the systems used by many retail clothing stores (covered in Chapter 5 of this guide).

Working in a clothing store (or in a shoe store or other retail store), even if only on a part-time or volunteer basis, is probably the best way to prepare yourself for opening your own bridal salon. Working for a time in a clothing store will give you valuable insight into pricing merchandise, what sells (and, equally important, what doesn't), how to deal with customers, how to arrange merchandise to its best advantage so that it looks attractive to buyers, and exactly what it takes to keep a store running smoothly on a day-to-day basis.

Visit the store you'd like to work in as a customer whenever possible before applying for a job so you can get to know the owner (and the store) a little. Remember, it will help if the owner recognizes you because you have been there before. Don't phone or write a letter; face to face works much better.

Here are some suggestions for introducing yourself and what you can do for a prospective employer:

- Explain that you are interested in learning retailing.

- Tell them if you've had any previous selling experience (whether it's shoes or ice cream).

- Think of some extra service you could offer, such as creating window displays.

- If no job is available and you really love the store and want to work there, volunteer to work for free. It could pay in the long run.

Finally, when applying for a job in a clothing store ensure that your demeanor, personality and dress reflect the qualities that you would be looking for in an employee. These characteristics are outlined in more detail in section 5.6.2 (*"Recruiting Staff"*).

> **TIP:** Almost any retail experience is valuable so apply to other retail stores if you can't find a job at a clothing store.

2.2.2 Get Volunteer Experience

One valuable way to get experience in fashion-related industries is to volunteer. Not only do you gain the kinds of insights you'll need to make your business a success, but you'll be able to give back to your community.

One simple way to get volunteer experience is to help friends or family members with their wedding or prom preparations. If you're interested in designing wedding dresses, try doing a few for friends (even if they're not planning to get married anytime soon). You can gain valuable experience in measuring clients, designing and building dresses, and fitting them, plus the additional experience of shopping for fabric, supplies and accessories.

You could also offer your services as a personal shopper, seamstress or even dress fitter to a high school in your area. Girls preparing for prom will be glad of your assistance. Another area you could look for volunteer opportunities is with your local religious or community organizations, either of which could provide referrals to connect your volunteer services with their members.

If you want experience helping women choose clothing that is flattering and appropriate for specific situations, try volunteering with a national organization like Dress for Success (**www.dressforsuccess.org**), or look for local charities in your area like Career Closet (**www.careercloset. org**), Working Wardrobes (**www.workingwardrobes.org**), or Wardrobe for Opportunity (**www.wardrobe.org**), located in California. These organizations provide donated business clothing to disadvantaged women who are trying to get into the workforce. Their volunteers help sort donated clothing, maintain donated clothing and the shops where it is kept, act as "personal shoppers" for the women in need of assistance, provide help with administrative duties, and much more.

You can also learn more about the different types of formal attire, and fitting them to different peoples' needs, by volunteering for organizations like Fairy Godmothers Inc. (**www.fairygodmothersinc.com**), Cinderella's Closet (**www.cinderellascloset.org**), and the Princess Project (**www.princessproject.org**), all of which provide prom dresses to girls from under-privileged families. If there is no similar project in your area, consider contacting your local volunteer center to suggest it.

You can also get involved with organizations like Brides Against Breast Cancer (**www.bridesagainstbreastcancer.org**), which collects donated wedding dresses for resale. The profits of the sales are then donated to help families of women with metastatic breast cancer. Visit **www. makingmemories.org** for more information on how you can volunteer to help set up, staff, and take down dress displays for the gown sales, which are regularly held in different cities across the United States.

The I Do Foundation is another nonprofit group that collects and resells wedding dresses. They donate the proceeds to charity and to the foundation's goals of encouraging wedding participants to make charitable donations. Visit **www.idofoundation.org** to learn more.

If these organizations don't have chapters in your area, consider starting one. Not only will you gain excellent experience and give back to your community, but you'll also create some instant publicity and good word-of-mouth advertising for your own bridal salon once you've got it started.

2.2.3   Work in the Wedding Industry

If you want to earn while you learn, try getting a job working for a wedding industry business. Some bridal salon owners we spoke with got their start as wedding planners, florists or other jobs in the wedding industry. The author of this guide is herself an experienced florist who has helped many brides with their floral arrangements.

The advantage of this work is that you get a first-hand look at how weddings function (especially working for caterers, photographers and DJs). You'll also get to meet lots of brides (especially working for florists, caterers or cake specialists and wedding planners). You'll get a sense of the dynamics of bridal parties, and you'll also get to see what the latest trends are by looking at the weddings you participate in and the trade magazines that come your way.

Plus, when you go ahead with your plans to open your own bridal salon, you'll have a ready source of referrals from your former employer.

2.2.4   Other Places to Learn

Fabric Stores

Working at a fabric store can give you insight into the types of textiles available. You'll have a chance to advise customers about suitable fabrics and patterns (whether they're for wedding outfits or not), and to become familiar with sewing terms, measurements and material choices.

Seamstresses and Tailors

When you start your own bridal salon you will hire or work with a seamstress or tailor. If you want to learn this aspect of the business, you could look for a part-time job as an assistant to a local seamstress or tailor, offer to volunteer or help out as an apprentice. This is a good way to learn about measuring, fitting and altering dresses to fit each bride perfectly.

You can often find contact information for local seamstresses by asking at a fabric store. They may have a bulletin board where people post their business cards, or the staff may be able to recommend a regular client who sews professionally. Keep in mind that seamstresses and tailors are often self-employed and may not have the time to show you everything, or the money to pay you to help. Offer your services in such a way that it could save them time or effort and you may create an enduring alliance that'll help your own salon in the future.

2.3 Be Your Own "Mystery Shopper"

You have probably heard of mystery shopping, where companies hire people to go into their various retail outlets and pose as shoppers. This is an excellent way for management to get feedback about what their retailers are doing wrong — and right. In order to take a first-hand look at how other people are running their own bridal salon you can become your own mystery shopper using these tips. You will find this information particularly helpful as you put together your business plan (see section 3.4) and marketing plans (section 6.1).

To begin, take a look in your local Yellow Pages under categories such as Bridal Salons, Wedding Apparel and Accessories, and Formal Attire. Take time to visit several stores that interest you. As you go to a number of stores and record your observations, a couple of things will begin to happen. First, you will begin to know what stores are in your area and which, if any, will be competition for you. Second, you will get a chance to see stores in action. There is no substitute for seeing first hand how bridal salons really run and operate.

"Shop your competitors then try to carry a line that no one else has. Look at their accessories, try to find other options. Do pick out floor layouts, and lighting that you like from competitors."

— Haley Hughes, En Vogue Events, Houston, TX

Take a small notebook and pen so you can discretely take notes. After you have been to each store, use a Store Impressions Form like the one on the pages that follow to record your observations.

TIP: As you assess local stores, remember that what you see there should simply serve as ideas. There are no hard and fast rules about what your own store must carry.

In addition to observing anonymously, getting a bridal salon owner's permission to let you observe them in action is also a wonderful way to learn. If you have a friend or a business contact that will let you spend a day seeing how they operate their business, it will be an excellent learning experience. In the next section you'll find advice on how to contact bridal salon owners.

Store Impressions Form

The Storefront

1. Is the store easy to spot from the street? ❑ Y ❑ N

2. Is it easy to park? ❑ Y ❑ N

3. Is there plenty of free parking or street parking? ❑ Y ❑ N

4. Is it an area with foot traffic? ❑ Y ❑ N

5. How is the area? ❑ Y ❑ N

6. What kinds of people do you see on the street? ❑ Y ❑ N

Entering the Shop

1. What do you notice about the atmosphere?

---

2. What do you like about the way the store looks?

3. What do you notice about the physical layout of the store?

4. Does the store seem inviting or uninviting? Why?

5. Is the store clean?   ❑ Y   ❑ N

6. Do you think you could get to a section   ❑ Y   ❑ N
   you were looking for without assistance?

The Staff

1. Are you greeted?   ❑ Y   ❑ N

2. Does the staff seem:

Welcoming?	❑ Y ❑ N	Grumpy?	❑ Y ❑ N
Pleasant?	❑ Y ❑ N	Pushy?	❑ Y ❑ N
Impatient?	❑ Y ❑ N		

3. When you ask a question, how do they respond?

4. Are they knowledgeable?   ❑ Y   ❑ N

5. Are you able to get your questions   ❑ Y   ❑ N
   answered to your satisfaction?

6. Does the staff make you feel comfortable   ❑ Y   ❑ N
   about asking a question?

Using the Store

1. Can you browse the selections easily? ❏ Y ❏ N

2. Are you comfortable? ❏ Y ❏ N

3. Is the fitting room clean and comfortable? ❏ Y ❏ N

4. Are the restrooms easily accessible and clean? ❏ Y ❏ N

5. How is the lighting?

6. Were you comfortable with the level of service when you were trying on gowns?

Merchandising

1. How is the merchandise arranged?

2. What is the quality of the merchandise?

3. What are the floor displays like?

4. Is the merchandise priced according to quality? ❏ Y ❏ N

5. Is there a separate section for custom work? ❏ Y ❏ N

Buying

1. Is the cash area organized? ❏ Y ❏ N

2. Is it easy to get served? ❏ Y ❏ N

3. Does the staff member speak pleasantly to you? ❏ Y ❏ N
4. Did you buy anything? ❏ Y ❏ N

Why or why not?

Leaving

1. What are your impressions when you leave?

2. Does a staff member notice you are leaving? ❏ Y ❏ N
3. Does anyone thank you? ❏ Y ❏ N
4. Does anyone say goodbye to you? ❏ Y ❏ N
5. Do you feel positive about your experience? ❏ Y ❏ N

Overall Impressions of the Store

1. What did you like best about the store?

2. What did you like the least?

3. What did you notice about the store's logo, bags or other printed material?

4. Will you go back to the store in the future? ❏ Y ❏ N
5. Will you recommend this store to anyone? ❏ Y ❏ N

2.4   Learn From Other Business Owners

Nothing compares to the experience of someone who's been there and done that. People who already own bridal salons can probably answer pretty much any question you might have. The tricky part can be approaching them in a way that lets them know you're not just asking in order to set up a competing store. The following section offers advice on how to navigate these kinds of discussions.

2.4.1   Talk to Bridal Salon Owners

After speaking with dozens of store owners, we recommend approaching bridal salon owners via e-mail, through an organization of business owners, or by driving to a non-competing store and asking their advice.

The bridal salon owners we spoke with were eager to offer advice and point out many additional resources. A good resource for finding other store owners is OneWed.com, an online wedding site that has searchable listings of bridal shops of all sorts across the U.S. Find them at **www. onewed.com/dresses/bridalshops.php**.

If you can get a store owner to talk to you, you can learn an amazing amount of insider information from someone who could be doing just what you want to do. Keep in mind, however, that while some may be quite willing to talk, others may be too busy. But if you ask nicely for information many people are very glad to share it.

> TIP: You will probably have a hard time if you approach a store owner who could be considered your direct competition. There is a difference between sharing knowledge and giving away trade secrets. Make sure that the experts you try to contact are not your direct competition.

So, how do you contact bridal salon owners? Try the following steps:

- Identify first what it is you are trying to accomplish

- Make a list of questions you want to ask

- Identify who you think you should talk to

- Make a list of contacts

- Take the steps to make contact (email, telephone, in person)

For example, let's assume you went to a great bridal salon in a neighboring town. First (after you have made your list of questions), find out the phone number and the owner's name. Then call and ask to speak to the owner. Here is a sample phone script:

"Hi, I am Bella Bryden. I was in your store while I was on vacation and I really enjoyed it. Could you tell me who the owner is? *(After you are connected to the owner, Ima Infogiver, you proceed.)*

"Hi, Ima Infogiver? My name is Bella Bryden and I am considering opening a bridal salon in another part of the state. I was on vacation and had a chance to stop in your store, and I loved it. *(Now, ask permission to ask — an old sales trick.)* I was wondering if you would be willing to let me ask you a couple questions about how you do things. I could use some expert advice."

TIP: It never hurts to tell experts you think they are experts. Most people like being recognized for their accomplishments.

Make an appointment to call back the store owner at their convenience. Then take some time and decide on a couple of questions you really want answers to. Ask only these questions. Also, offer to correspond with your contact using email if the expert prefers this. Always thank the expert for their time and make sure they know you appreciate the information. If you build this relationship slowly you can ask for more help and advice, and perhaps you can even find a mentor.

Remember to:

- Ask permission to ask questions

- Be sensitive to the expert's time

- Decide ahead of time what you will ask

- Don't overwhelm your expert with too many questions

- Build the relationship slowly and ask for more time at a later date

As you do research on the Internet, you will undoubtedly begin to see bridal salon websites that interest you. All of these sites have contact information you can use to directly ask for help and advice.

Remember to adhere to the same advice in email that you would use on the phone. Be courteous, brief, and grateful. Don't worry if you have to send out a number of letters before you have a response. Bridal salon owners are busy people. If you are polite and persistent, some store owners will be willing to talk to you.

2.4.2 Join an Association

Bridal Salon Associations

Association for Wedding Professionals International

Website: **www.afwpi.com**

To learn more about the bridal salon industry, consider joining the Association for Wedding Professionals International. You can join as a regular member for $240 annually (at the time of publication). This membership entitles you to a newsletter and directory listings, and allows you to take part in member conferences where you can attend workshops and fashion shows and meet other bridal salon owners. You'll also get special discounts from associate members such as Avis car rental, as well as discounts on insurance and bridal show booth rentals.

American Wedding Association

Website: **www.americanweddingassociation.com**

You can also join the American Wedding Association, a professional organization for all those involved in the wedding industry. Becoming a member is as simple as paying $70 (at the time of publication) and agreeing to abide by the organization's code of ethics. Members enjoy a regular newsletter, advertising promotions, and access to the members-only portion of the organization's website, which includes information about businesses for sale, articles about various aspects of the bridal industry, and more.

Bridal Association of America

Website: **www.bridalassociationofamerica.com/membership**

The Bridal Association of America offers its members benefits such as networking, website hosting, insurance discounts and listings in a variety of directories. There are several levels of membership depending on whether you want to be listed in local, regional or national directories.

Once you're an established store owner, it's a good idea to join a national or state association because membership gives customers confidence to see the Association's logo displayed in your place of business. Another benefit is the networking that takes place.

2.4.3 More Informal Learning Resources

Online

Another good source of acquiring information from experts is through online message boards like The Knot. Here you can meet with actual brides and store owners and ask questions of your own or read through the posts. You can also get insight into customers and what they are looking for.

- *The Knot*
  http://community.theknot.com/cs/ks/community/

- *Wedding Bells Magazine*
  (Canadian bridal magazine with an online discussion board. At the link below, click on "Forums.")
  www.weddingbells.ca

Business Organizations

You can also join a number of excellent organizations designed for business owners to learn and network in an organized setting. One excellent resource is your local Chamber of Commerce. Chambers usually have an annual fee and are set up to aid the local businessperson with a variety of business-related issues. Members attend local meetings and can also take part in events designed to help them be more successful.

To find out how to contact your local chamber, visit the national websites. For the U.S. Chamber of Commerce visit **www.uschamber.com/chambers/directory/default.htm?d=false**. For the Canadian Chamber of Commerce Directory visit **www.chamber.ca/index.php/en/links/C57**.

2.5 Take a Course

Learning to be a bridal salon owner isn't a simple matter of getting a degree and knowing how to do it. In fact, you don't need any formal education to learn how to become a bridal salon owner. As Susan Alexander Shapiro, founder of BravoBride, says, "It was trial by fire. My only training was planning my own wedding." Like Shapiro, you can chart your own course when it comes to learning this business.

To start, you might consider taking courses that will enhance your skills and knowledge in areas related to running a bridal salon. For example, you might want to brush up on some basic skills such as retail display, which will let you create beautiful in-store and window displays. You'll also find sewing skills handy, especially if you will offer alterations and fittings in your store. Plus, knowing how to replace buttons or fix zippers is an invaluable skill when you're dealing with sample wedding gowns that may be tried on many times in a row.

A knowledge of fabric care, which includes skills like knowing how to get out minor stains and pressing pleats, will also be helpful, as you may occasionally need to touch up your merchandise after a try-on or fitting session. You can take courses on fashion merchandising and sewing at many community colleges, and many fabric stores also offer basic sewing and needlework classes.

Business Courses

Another area in which you might need a bit more knowledge is the business end of running a bridal salon. Earning a degree, diploma, or certificate in business can be helpful in running your own business, though this is not strictly necessary. However, if you don't have any background in running a business, you should seriously consider some formal education. If you do want to brush up on some business skills, you can find links to colleges and universities at Peterson's Planner at **www.petersons.com**, or in Canada you can visit the SchoolFinder website at **www.schoolfinder.com**.

However, a formal business education is not necessary to run a bridal salon. There are many successful business owners who are self-taught and have never studied business.

Others have taken a course here and there but do not possess a degree. However, the skills you learn in business classes can come in handy. Depending on which of your skills you would like to develop, consider taking courses on topics such as:

- Advertising

- Basic Accounting

- Business Communications

- Business Management

- Entrepreneurship

- Merchandising

- Retailing

Your local college or university may offer these and other business courses. Through the continuing education department you may be able to take a single course on a Saturday or over several evenings. If you can't find a listing for the continuing education department in your local phone book, call the college's main switchboard and ask for the continuing education department. They will be able to tell you about upcoming courses.

If you are not interested in attending courses at a school, or you don't have the time, another option that can easily fit into your schedule is distance learning. Traditionally these were called correspondence courses and the lessons were mailed back and forth between student and instructor. Today, with the help of the Internet, there are many on-line courses available. Again, check your local community college, university, or business school to see if they offer online courses.

Your local Chamber of Commerce may also offer training courses and seminars for new business owners. Many also offer consultations with re-tired executives and business owners who are well-qualified to offer advice. Visit **www.chamberofcommerce.com** to find a Chamber near you.

2.6 Resources for Self-Study

Of course, it's not necessary to go to school to learn much of what you'll need to know for running a successful bridal salon. You can learn about the wedding industry and wedding fashions by attending trade shows, participating in online discussion forums, reading books and even watching television shows. This section outlines some of the many free or low-cost resources available to you for your own self-study.

2.6.1 Bridal Expos and Markets

As a future bridal salon owner, you can also attend events like these, gathering information about the salons displaying their wares. You can ask questions or meet bridal salon owners from other areas who may be willing to offer you information. To find out when a bridal show is scheduled for your area, contact your local Chamber of Commerce. You can also ask your local bridal salons, florists or caterers, all of whom are likely to have booths at the next event.

Bridal Expos

Bridal expos are two to three days in duration and can attract up to 10,000 visitors a day. One of the largest is The Great Bridal Expo, which sponsors events in cities around the country. The link below will take you to their latest tour schedule. The other links will help you find local bridal shows.

- *The Great Bridal Expo*
  www.greatbridalexpo.com/tourschedule.aspx

- *Bridal Show Producers International*
  www.bspishows.com

- *Bridal Shows*
  www.weddingdetails.com/shows

- *Association of Bridal Consultants*
  www.bridalassn.com

- *The Association for Wedding Professionals International*
  http://afwpi.com/wedproconferences/Gowns.html

Bridal Markets

In addition to consumer-oriented bridal shows, the wedding industry thrives on bridal markets, trade and fashion shows where retailers can see the newest trends and samples of merchandise first-hand. By attending bridal markets, you'll not only become familiar with the range of new merchandise that's available, but you'll get to meet wholesalers, designers, suppliers and other bridal salon owners (as well as many other wedding industry professionals) all in one place. You can ask questions, take home samples and collect business contacts, all of which means attending trade shows can be one of the most efficient ways of learning more about this industry.

One of the industry's premier events for bridal wear is the National Bridal Market Chicago. This is where manufacturers and wholesalers present their new collections, hold fashion shows and network with each other. You can find out more at **http://nationalbridalmarket.com/the-show**.

2.6.2 Books

Amazon.com lists more than 300,000 books on the subject of weddings, but of course you do not have the time to read them all! So here is a selection of excellent books you may want to start with. Look for them at your local library, browse through them at a local bookstore, or order them online.

- *Beautiful Bridal Accessories You Can Make,*
  by Jacquelynne Johnson

- *Bridal Couture: Fine Sewing Techniques for Wedding Gowns and Evening Wear,*
  by Susan Khalje

- *Brides, Inc.: American Weddings and the Business of Tradition,*
  by Vicki Howard

- *Couture Sewing Techniques,*
  by Claire B. Schaeffer

- *A Designer's Book of Bridal Gowns,*
  by Debby Roosa

- *The Knot Book of Wedding Gowns,*
  by Carley Roney

- *The Perfect Wedding Dress,*
  by Philip Delamore

- *Sew a Beautiful Wedding,*
  by Gail Brown and Karen Dillon

2.6.3   Websites

Throughout this guide you will find numerous websites that can assist you in various aspects of starting and running a bridal salon. In this section, we focus on several key resources that can help you quickly increase your business knowledge. Each of these websites is a wealth of information that you can refer to throughout the process of starting your business.

Starting a Business Sites

SBA

The Small Business Administration (SBA) is a leading U.S. government resource for information about licensing, taxes, and starting a small business. You can find a range of resources including information on financing your new business, business plans and much more at **www.sbaonline.sba.gov**.

SCORE

The Service Corps of Retired Executives (SCORE) is an organization of U.S. volunteers who donate their time and expertise to new business owners. You can find information on taxes, tips for starting your business, or even find a mentor who will coach you and help you maximize your chances of succeeding as a new business owner. Visit them at **www.score.org**.

Canada Business Service Centers

This Canadian government website offers information on legislation, taxes, incorporation, and other issues of interest to Canadian business owners or those who do business in Canada. For more information and a list of services they offer visit their website at **www.canadabusiness.ca**.

Industry Sites

If you type "weddings" into a search engine, you will have literally thousands of websites to choose from. So here's a short list of the best websites for getting started learning about the bridal industry. The following sites either provide detailed information, or links to detailed information, on numerous aspects of wedding gowns and wedding vendors.

- *The Knot*
  Offers articles, advice, planning tools and more for brides-to-be and wedding professionals as well.
  www.theknot.com

- *Association of Bridal Consultants*
  Information, networking and advice for wedding professionals and vendors.
  www.bridalassn.com

- *Association for Wedding Professionals International*
  Offers information and assistance to wedding professionals, links to bridal show producers, a free e-newsletter, information about conferences and trade shows and much more.
  http://afwpi.com/

- *American Wedding Association*
  Offers advice, networking and job opportunities for wedding industry professionals. Membership required; apply online.
  www.americanweddingassociation.com/

- *Wedding Industry*
  The best place on the web to get real-life advice on all aspects of running a bridal salon. Access to this online forum is free, but you must apply for membership with an explanation of why you want to join.
  www.weddingindustry.com

- *The Wedding Planners Institute of Canada*
  Useful advice and information for Canadian wedding industry professionals, plus courses in wedding planning.
  www.wpic.ca

2.6.4 Magazines

Magazines are a great way to keep up to date on the trends in wedding fashions, and to pay attention to changes that affect the bridal industry. Many of these magazines also offer a large online component with blogs and reader forums. Some magazines to look for both in print and online include the following:

- *Vows: The Bridal and Wedding Business Journal*
  The premier trade magazine for wedding professionals. Not available on newsstands. Website has downloadable archive of articles available for $4.50 each.
  www.vowsmagazine.com

- *Martha Stewart Weddings*
  America's tastemaker has a popular say on weddings, too.
  www.marthastewartweddings.com

- *Wedding Bells Magazine*
  Focuses on Canadian weddings and brides.
  www.weddingbells.ca/

- *Brides*
  Wedding fashions, planning and photographs in the magazine. The website offers much more, including blogs, weekly newsletters and an online forum.
  www.brides.com

- *Bridal Guide Magazine*
  Advice on wedding planning, fashion, and more. Its website also offers blogs and an online forum.
  www.bridalguide.com

3. Starting Your Bridal Salon

Now that we've looked at ways to develop your business skills, it's time to look at how to go about actually starting your own store. This chapter of the guide will walk you step-by-step through the process.

Use the checklist below as a guideline to help you complete the steps necessary to get your business going. In fact, you may want to print the checklist and keep it nearby as you go through the rest of this guide so you can add items as you learn more about them.

Getting Started Basics Checklist

- Choose your niche.

- Prepare your business plan.

- Obtain a business license.

- Locate several potential locations and weigh pros and cons of each.

- Secure financing.

- Lease or purchase store space.

- Obtain any necessary permits or certificates.

- Purchase store fixtures.

- Purchase software your store will use for inventory.

- Decide what merchandise you will offer for sale, locate suppliers and purchase inventory.

- Start advertising your grand opening.

- Decide if you need help. Interview and hire additional employees, if necessary.

- If you are planning to hire employees, obtain an Employee Identification Number (contact details later in this guide).

- Complete your store operations manual and finalize any store policies.

- Make a plan for your grand opening.

- Set up systems for record keeping.

- Set up window displays.

- Open your business.

3.1 Choosing Your Niche

"Know your market! Every city is different. In Seattle, there is a ton of money (Microsoft, Boeing, tons of biochemical companies), but it is understated, unlike New York or LA. People like things to be fabulous, but not in a really showy, dripping-with-crystals way. Every town has a different character and every market niche has its own flavor—figure out which one you want to go after and do it well. Don't try to be everything to everybody."

— Daniela Isabella/Ferdico Faget,
Bella Signature Design Inc., Seattle

The first thing to consider for your store is what types of products and services you will offer. This is your "niche" or specialty. As the quote above suggests, an important component of deciding on your niche is to know your market.

To help you choose your niche you'll need to do some market research to give you an idea of trends in the industry you are entering. You'll need to answer the following questions:

- Is there a need in your community for what you plan to sell?

- Can you effectively compete?

The best place to start is by studying other successful stores similar to the one you are planning to open. Don't be afraid to ask other retail store owners for their advice. You may hear that sales of certain types of products are booming, while some products may be losing popularity.

Also find out if any stores similar to yours have opened or closed in the area recently. If you're new to the area, you may have to speak to other business owners and locals to get this information. While your marketing and customer service might be better than the stores that closed, the fact that a similar store has been unsuccessful might indicate that a particular type of retail outlet doesn't do well in your area. If at all possible, try to track down the previous store owner through the local phone book and ask a few questions.

You'll find some additional resources for doing market research in section 3.4 on business planning to help you focus in on your market, but even if you already have an idea of your specialty, this section may help you refine it further.

Initially, as you consider what niche to fill with your own store, remember that the simplest approach is to sell something you are familiar with. Look at areas of your life and experience to help you decide. Stick with what is familiar at first, but don't make your store's niche too narrow in your first year. Starting with a wider range of products and services will help you adapt to the needs of your clientele. Over time you will likely find some products and services are more profitable for you, and you can change your offerings as you learn more about what your customers want.

3.1.1   Upscale or Couture Gown Store

Catering to exclusive customers with unique designer wear, an upscale bridal salon carries only the most exclusive gowns by a selection of well-known or up-and-coming designers. Couture gowns are custom-made for each bride and their price tags reflect that individualized attention to detail.

If you are in an area with many society weddings or can realistically anticipate catering to clients for whom money is no object, consider a couture gown boutique. Remember, though, that you'll need to buy samples from the designers you carry, an investment that represents a larger initial financial outlay.

3.1.2   Bridesmaid and Formalwear Store

"Look at everyday clothing women are wearing. Is your town more conservative, or fashion forward? Stocking your boutique with bridesmaid dresses that complement the fashion taste of the women where you live will attract them to your store over others."

— Keri Chantler and Jenni Hailer,
Twirl Boutique, Scottsdale, AZ

Gone are the days when bridesmaids had to wear the most unflattering dresses the bride could find! Bridesmaids are now breathing sighs of relief to know there is a growing number of salons, such as Twirl Boutique, that are catering especially to them. With fashionable cocktail-style dresses and outfits that flatter rather than embarrass, bridesmaid boutiques are capturing a segment of the formalwear market, too. They can also provide flower girl dresses, prom dresses and dresses for quinceañera events (Latin American celebrations of a girl's 15th birthday).

Dresses for bridesmaids and flower girls are generally custom-order gowns. The bride usually picks a dress for her attendants based on the color scheme and theme of her wedding (e.g. daytime vs. evening, modern vs. traditional). Once a dress is selected, the bridesmaids and flower girls are measured, and custom-made dresses are ordered from the manufacturer.

TIP: Many designers offer the same dress style with different sleeve, neckline, and skirt options. This allows for each attendant to choose a flattering style for her figure, while maintaining a consistent look for the entire bridal party.

Many modern brides opt for off-the-rack, cocktail-style bridesmaid dresses that attendants can wear again for other occasions. To meet this demand, bridal boutiques often stock an inventory of off-the-rack cocktail dresses in popular styles and colors. These can double as prom dresses or formalwear so you can expand your target market.

3.1.3 Ethnic Wedding Store

Many parts of North America are becoming more culturally diverse, and the wedding industry is responding to the opportunities that come with these changes. If you live in an area where there is a large population of people from a particular ethnic group, you might consider opening a salon that specializes in the types of gowns that are worn by brides from that group.

For example, salons catering to Orthodox Jews offer "modest" gowns that are gorgeous and fashionable, but cover the bride's arms and shoulders in accordance with tradition. Contact your local, state or provincial government's vital statistics department to learn more about the ethnic demographics of your area, and open a salon that caters to culturally specific weddings. The U.S. Census website is also a good place to find this information. Try **www.census.gov/population/www/pop-profile/ profile_list.html** as a start.

It will help if you (or a staff member) belong to the cultural group you're catering to, as this will give you insights into traditions and contacts within the community that will help grow your business. Catering to a particular ethnic group can also be a sideline in a more traditional bridal salon operation.

3.1.4 Custom Design Gown Salon

If you've always had a knack for designing and sewing original garments, consider opening a custom design gown salon. You'll be able to provide unique, one-of-a-kind works of art for your clients to wear on their wedding day, and to cherish afterwards. By choosing your custom designs, your clients will know they're getting something as special as they are, and will be assured of its perfect fit.

Because you're making the gowns in-house (or hiring a talented seamstress to do your sewing for you), you'll keep more control over both the production process and the production costs. This translates into a greater potential profit for you, because you'll eliminate the middleman of factory production and distribution.

3.1.5   Second-hand Gown Salon

Many brides today are looking for ways to both economize and be more environmentally friendly. In fact, "green" weddings have been named by many of the experts we've talked to as one of the fastest-growing trends in the industry. You can catch the green wave by recycling wedding gowns and bridesmaids' dresses at a second-hand gown salon.

Consider offering dresses on consignment (in which brides bring their used-but-still-perfect dresses for sale at your store and you take a percentage of the sale price). You might also consider buying used gowns outright, which allows you to make alterations, add embellishments or even simply use the material to recycle something old into something new.

3.1.6   Plus-Size Bridal

Half of all American women are size 14 or larger. With this in mind, more and more designers are recognizing the untapped potential of the plus-size bridal market. Research what local competitors are offering to plus-size brides. If you don't want to jump into the market blind, experiment by adding more plus-size styles to your sample selection to gauge the demand for plus-size bridal in your area.

3.1.7   Other Specialties

"Rent tuxedos in your bridal studio. It is a safe, inexpensive, no-overhead piece of revenue."

> — Lillie Garrido, White Couture Designer Bridal
> and Tuxedos, Park City, UT

There are a number of other types of bridal merchandise you could consider. Bridal boutiques can generate significant revenue by selling favors, place cards and other low-cost wedding paraphernalia. Generally, these items can be purchased wholesale for a low cost and sold at a healthy margin.

Examples of these miscellaneous items include place cards, guest books, disposable cameras for the tables, flower-girl baskets, ring-bearer pillows, and gifts for members of the wedding party.

Bridal lingerie includes garments for brides to wear as foundation garments under their wedding gowns and to wear as nightwear on their wedding night and honeymoon. Wedding shoes are crucial for going with that perfect dress. Accessories such as veils, tiaras, earrings, purses and garters add a special something to complete an outfit. And men's formalwear is another option to consider, whether it's a tuxedo rental service or a full line of men's wedding outfits.

3.2 Options for Starting a Bridal Salon

Once you have decided on your niche, you'll need to decide whether to buy an existing store or open a new store. Deciding which route is right for you is an important decision.

An established store will cost more than starting from scratch, but it also comes with customers, inventory, and reputation, which means it's likely to continue with its pre-established success. A new store typically costs less to start up, and you can tailor it specifically to your own vision. Unlike buying an established store, though, you will need to spend more on advertising, gaining clientele, and making a reputation for your business — and new businesses have a higher risk of failure.

3.2.1 Buying an Established Store

One way to start is to buy an existing business and make it your own. Buying an existing store can show you a profit on the very first day you're open. You'll still need a business plan, financing, a lawyer and an accountant, but many of the other decisions – like what to call it and where to locate it — will already be made. In addition, you will acquire all or most of the equipment, furniture, supplies, and inventory you will need to get started. You also get clientele and the established business name.

However, you should also look very careful at whatever else you might be acquiring. The business may have outstanding debts and you may have to assume any liabilities that come with the store, such as bills it owes to its suppliers, or repairs or maintenance expenditures that haven't been paid.

If this option for starting your business appeals to you, begin by looking for stores for sale in your area. Do not be afraid to approach local store owners and inquire if they are interested in selling their business, or if they know any store owners considering retirement. And, don't forget to look in your local newspaper, local business publications, and contact the Chamber of Commerce for information on shops that may possibly be for sale.

What to Look for Before You Buy

Purchasing an existing business can be a good way to get into the retail trade immediately, but there are a few cautions. You could be purchasing a failed business with a poor financial history, bad reputation, or even some hidden liabilities as mentioned earlier. You need to perform a due diligence investigation, meaning you need to look at the operations of the business, including revenues, cash flow, assets and liabilities, licensing, and so on, before purchasing.

To protect yourself, before making a deal for any business hire an accountant to go over the company's books. This will help you to determine if the seller is representing the business accurately and honestly. Then, before signing an Agreement of Purchase and Sale, you should enlist the services of a lawyer to review the written agreement.

Following are a few things to look for as you start your search for an existing business to buy.

Why the Business is For Sale

Here are a few of the most common reason why business owners offer their businesses for sale:

- The owner is retiring or has health problems

- The owner is moving on to another store or another business altogether

- The business has failed and the owner wants to get out as quickly as possible

- The owner is afraid of increasing competition

- One key element of their business strategy is faulty, such as the type of inventory offered

- The business is part of a chain and is not doing as well as other stores owned by the same company

- A partnership has fallen apart and the partners are liquidating all or a part of the company's assets

Before purchasing an existing retail business answer the following important questions (with assistance from the seller whenever possible).

- Why is the vendor selling the business?

- What is the sales history of the store?

- What is the average cost to maintain the store?

- What assets or liabilities will come with the purchase?

- Are there any tax, legal or property issues you will have to contend with?

The previous owner may help you with many of these issues or you may have to do your own research, perhaps by consulting local government, realtors or other merchants. Whatever the situation, you should never buy an existing business without knowing all of the details.

You should have complete access to the previous owner's store records, including financial statements. With these you will have information about the customer base and noticeable patterns in the store's business practices. Unwillingness by the previous owner to provide financial statements for your complete inspection might be a tip-off that something isn't right with the business.

Potential buyers often work in the store for a short time before purchasing it. Owners are often willing to train the buyer. If the business owner you are thinking about buying from is unwilling to do this, you should find out why.

Hidden Costs

When you purchase an established business it seems like you're purchasing a turnkey operation with license, location, traffic and inventory all in place and you just have to open the doors. However, there may be hidden expenses that you will have to pay for, such as back taxes, needed repairs or building code violations, so be sure to watch for these. You don't want an angry supplier showing up at your door demanding money for inventory purchased by the previous owner but never paid for. (You've already purchased the inventory from the owner and now you'll have to pay for it a second time.)

In addition to paying for the business, and any miscellaneous expenses, you will also need money to pay for equipment and supplies, and additional inventory. You may also want to start a marketing campaign in order to make people aware of the fact that you're the new owner and let the community know that you're open for business. This is particularly important if you've bought a business that might have been on the decline for whatever reasons.

Finally, if you plan to remodel a store after buying it, perhaps to give it a fresh new image, then that could easily become another significant expense depending on the size of the job and the contractor you hire. Keep all these additional potential costs in mind as you consider buying the existing business.

Creating a Spec Sheet

A spec sheet is a summary of the business and includes the book value (total assets minus total liabilities and goodwill), market value (the book value figure adjusted to reflect the current market value of assets), and the liquidation value (how much the owner could raise if the business was liquidated). Earnings potential should also be considered.

If the value you arrive at is significantly different from what the owner is asking for the business, ask the seller how he or she arrived at the price. You can then make your offer based on your estimate of worth and the owner's asking price. You don't need to accept that the business is actually worth what the owner thinks it is.

The real worth of a business is in its continuing profitability, so examine the financial records closely (especially the profit and loss statements and cash flow statements) to get a good idea of what your revenue would be, as well as your expenses and net income. Try to buy a business for its annual profit. Don't be distracted by the listed price.

One helpful resource is the Due Diligence Checklist at FindLaw.com. The full website address is **http://smallbusiness.findlaw.com/starting-business** (click on "More Topics", then on "Buying an Existing Business" then on "Due Diligence Checklist" under Tools & Resources). This checklist shows you everything that you should check out about any business you're thinking of purchasing in areas like the business's organization and good standing, financial statements, physical assets, real estate, and much more. Be sure to consult this checklist or one like it as you perform your due diligence investigation.

The Canada Business Services for Entrepreneurs website has an excellent page at **http://bsa.canadabusiness.ca/gol/bsa/site.nsf/en/su06889. html#a4** (click on "How to Buy a Business - Checklist"), that details everything you need to consider when purchasing an existing business. Information includes advice on how to determine asset and earnings value, how to valuate a business and a detailed list of questions to ask when looking at a business you're thinking of purchasing.

Purchase Price

Purchase prices are determined by a number of factors. These include region and neighborhood location, profit and local economy, potential growth, and the owner's own sense of what the company is worth based on reputation or goodwill. BusinessesforSale.com, Business Nation, Biz BuySell.com and others offer listings of many types of businesses that, for whatever reason, are being offered for sale. These sites list each business's asking price, and usually state its turnover and profit.

Expect to pay from $50,000 to upwards of $150,000 for an existing bridal salon or boutique. This usually will include all contents of the shop and often means taking over an existing lease or rental agreement for the location. Starting your own store requires a lot of energy and devotion — whether you build from scratch or buy an existing store. You should plan on waiting two to five years to earn back your purchase price.

Recent listings of bridal salon businesses for sale on these websites included:

A popular shop in a Chicago suburb that has been in business for more than 40 years, employs a staff of seven part-time employees, and is the only bridal salon in its area. It had an annual revenue of $435,000, with a net profit of $50,000. The asking price of $49,000 included all shop fixtures, but $139,000 in inventory was extra.

A 10 year old bridal and formalwear boutique located on a busy shopping strip in a small town in southern California. The annual sales revenue of this owner-operated shop was $100,000, and net profit was $50,000. For the asking price of $65,000, the store included all fixtures and inventory, a value of $30,000. The seller would also provide two weeks of training to the buyer.

A 3,000-square-foot, upscale full-service bridal salon north of Boston, with an annual revenue of $750,000. The asking price of $349,000 included $275,000 worth of stock and inventory, including custom and off-the-rack brides' and bridesmaids' gowns, and a wide selection of accessories.

- *BusinessesForSale.com*
  (Includes business for sale in the U.S., Canada, U.K. and other countries)
  www.businessesforsale.com

- *Business Nation*
  www.businessnation.com/Businesses_for_Sale/

- *BizQuest*
  www.bizquest.com/buy

- *BizBen (California only)*
  www.bizben.com

Try entering the keywords "bridal wear"; "gown salon"; "wedding apparel" and "formal wear" into each website's search engine or search by industry.

> **TIP:** Beware of websites that require a fee or ask for personal information to view their listings. Real Estate agents make their money on sales and not on people browsing.

Financing

Some owners will allow you to finance an existing business if you can come up with a good down payment but are unable to purchase it outright. Many of the owners of the businesses for sale at the websites above are willing to negotiate financing with potential buyers. Be sure you understand the terms of any financing you set up with the seller. See a lawyer before agreeing to anything.

If you are considering borrowing from a lending institution such as a bank then financing an existing, profitable business is much less of a risk than starting a new one. A lending institution will want to see your detailed business plan before agreeing to lend you any money. (See section 3.4 for more on how to write a business plan, and section 3.5 for more about financing your new business venture.)

Making an Offer

When you have done your research, figured out what the business is worth and decided you want to buy the business you may then decide to make an offer, possibly less than the asking price based on your own valuation of the business. Usually the owner then will make a counter-offer. Keep in mind that you may have less leeway to negotiate a better purchase price if the owner will be financing the purchase for you.

You will usually be asked to pay a non-refundable deposit. This is standard and ensures the owner that you are a serious buyer. Be sure to get a deposit receipt and get any purchase agreement in writing after you've arrived at a mutually agreeable price. Also be sure that every important detail about the purchase is mentioned in the contract. Because so much money is at risk, a lawyer should draw up or at least review the contract before either party signs.

Buying an Existing Building

A second option rather than buying an entire business is to buy an existing building in which to set up shop and then move your business into it. The obvious advantage here is that buying an existing building often is less expensive than buying an established business along with the building housing it. Another aspect to consider is that, as already mentioned, if you buy an existing business you inherit both advantages and disadvantages from the previous owner.

One advantage of buying a building is that it most likely has already passed fire and building codes, unlike a new project that will require inspections and approval by municipal authorities before you can occupy it. Be sure to check first with zoning laws to be sure you're safe to operate your business there.

There are disadvantages as well. The building may require heavy infrastructure repairs (such as utilities or plumbing) or you might have to completely remodel the interior. Repair and remodeling costs can be expensive, even into thousands of dollars, so be sure to inspect the building carefully for any structural problems before you buy it.

Do a thorough investigation of the building's interior and exterior. Check the electrical systems, cooling and ventilation systems, bathrooms, walls and ceilings. If possible, interview the previous owner and ask about any potential problems that might create extra costs for you.

You should consider hiring a building inspector to conduct a thorough, professional evaluation of the property. Hiring a professional building inspector, though an added cost to buying a building, could save you from a disastrous purchase (and thousands of dollars in repairs) so consider finding one to look at any property you're thinking about purchasing. To find building inspectors in your area, check the Yellow Pages under "Building Inspection Service."

3.2.2 Opening a New Bridal Salon

Of course, you can always start from scratch and open a brand new store. That way, you can have complete control over every step of the process and make sure that your shop is everything you want it to be. The information in the rest of this chapter will show you how to do just that.

3.3   Choosing a Store Name

If you decide to start up your own store from square one, choosing a name may be one of the most important decisions you make for your new business. You want something catchy that will draw people into the store while clearly indicating it is a bridal salon.

If you have the financial resources, you could hire a naming professional to help you choose the right name for your company. Known as name consultants or naming firms, these organizations are experts at creating names, and can help you with trademark laws.

> **TIP:**   Business names don't have to be trademarked, but having them trademarked prevents anyone else from using the same name. Trademark laws are complicated, so if you think you want your company name trademarked it's a good idea to consult a lawyer with expertise in that area.

Most people starting up a new retail store, however, don't have the money necessary to hire professional name consultants. The cost of these services can start at a few thousand dollars. Instead, to come up with a name yourself, consider your niche and what types of customers you are trying to reach. You might even hold a brainstorming session and enlist family and friends for suggestions. If somebody comes up with a really good one, you'll probably know it right away. Here are name samples from the store owners we surveyed.

- Shades of White

- I Do, I Do

- Simply Elegant Bridal Boutique

- P.W. Jitters Bridal Boutique

- Dream Weddings

In most jurisdictions, once you have chosen your business name you will also have to file a "Doing Business As" (DBA) application, to register the fictitious name under which you will conduct your business operations. The DBA allows you to operate under a name other than your own legal name.

Filing a DBA usually takes place at the county level, although some states require that you file at the state level, publish your intent to operate under an assumed business name, and sign an affidavit stating that you have done so. However, in most cases it's usually just a short form to fill out and a small filing fee that you pay to your state or provincial government. You can find links at the Business.gov website to the appropriate government departments where you can file your business name at **www.business.gov/register/business-name/dba.html**.

Trademarked Business Names

A trademark database lists all registered and trademarked business names. In the U.S., the essential place to start is with the U.S. Patent and Trademark Office. You can hire a company that specializes in this type of service to do a name search for you, if you choose. However, you can do an online search of the federal trademark database yourself to determine whether a name has already been registered.

You can also do this at the county level or at the state level when you file for a DBA using the fictitious names database of the agency you're filing with. The fictitious names database is where non-trademarked business names are listed.

You can check trademarks at the United States Patent and Trademark Office (**www.uspto.gov/main/trademarks.htm**). In Canada, the default database for name searches is the Newly Upgraded Automated Name Search (NUANS). You can search the NUANS database at **www.nuans. com**. There is a $20 charge for each NUANS search.

If you would like to learn more about this subject, you can read an in-depth article about naming your business entitled "How to Name Your Business" at the Entrepreneur.com website. This article includes tips on how to brainstorm ideas for naming your business, as well as establishing trademarks and how to file a DBA. A related article, "8 Mistakes to Avoid When Naming Your Business" offers tips on avoiding some typical business naming mistakes. You can learn about other issues to be aware of when naming your business, at the Business.gov website. Visit **www.business.gov/register/business-name/** to find additonal advice.

3.4 Your Business Plan

Many business owners fail not because their business ideas weren't great but rather because of their lack of planning. A business plan is a detailed breakdown of every aspect of your business, including its location, sources of start-up funding, aspects of financial planning and an in-depth description of your proposed business. A good business plan serves two purposes. It's your guide (one that can be used and modified as necessary on an ongoing basis) for how you want your company to progress and grow.

Your business plan also serves as a sales tool should you decide to seek outside funding for your business. A business plan is essential in meeting with your bank manager or other lending institution. They need to know you are a good risk before they loan you money. A business plan tells them that you are prepared and know where you're going.

Additionally, a well-thought out plan will help you to identify any factors that will affect your profits and your competitive advantages. A business plan will allow you to step back from your excitement about starting a business, and take an objective look at your plans.

A good plan will help you over the rough spots by identifying where you might have slow cash flow during certain seasons (e.g., during the summer when many people are away vacationing). A well-prepared plan will help you learn who your customers and competition are, to understand the strengths and weaknesses of your business, and to recognize factors that could affect the growth of your company.

You shouldn't treat your business plan as if its contents are written in stone, however. There are many reasons why you'll want to keep up-to-date with your business plan. As your business changes and grows, your business plan probably will need some tweaking to reflect new goals and changing customer purchasing patterns, for example. (You might find that certain products sell better than others as you move forward.) Your business plan description will need to change if you branch out into a different product niche in your store.

In the next section, we'll guide you through the various elements of your business plan and how they fit into the overall conception of your new enterprise.

3.4.1   What To Include In a Business Plan

A business plan can be a simple description of your business concept or a detailed report, including graphs and charts of potential growth. A typical business plan should include the following items. You will learn more about a number of the important items, such as marketing and store operations, later in this guide.

Cover Page

The cover page should list your name, home address, phone number and any other contact information you wish to provide. This is an often-overlooked, yet essential, piece of the business plan. If you are presenting your plan to investors or the bank, they must know how to contact you.

Executive Summary

This should be an upbeat explanation of your overall concept. Think of the paragraphs on the backs of book covers. An executive summary encapsulates the major contents of your business plan just as the paragraphs summarize the plot of a book. You want to sell your idea, so you need to keep it positive.

You should write the Executive Summary after the rest of the sections are completed (except, of course, the Table of Contents). The Executive Summary is the synopsis of your business vision. It should be concise and explain the major contents of your business plan.

Be sure to include the following important points:

- Business start date and location
- Financial objectives for the year
- Commitment to resources (inventory, facilities, staff)
- Products and services
- A strong closing statement

Table of Contents

Make it easy for your investors by including a Table of Contents so they can easily turn to specific items such as your profit projections. A Table of Contents, although it's the first thing to appear in the plan, should be the last thing you write. That way you already have all the content and page numbers in place.

Description

The description of your business should cover the products and services you plan to offer and be as specific as possible. You can also include industry information about other retail stores in your niche market.

In this section of your business plan, you will include the following:

- *Products and Services:* What type of merchandise and services you will be offering to customers and any additional product lines or services you hope to add.

- *Customers:* This is the section to give an overview of who you think your typical customers will be.

- *Goals:* What would you like to achieve by opening your store? To establish yourself as a specialist in a certain sector of the industry? Expand your store to a larger operation in five years? Describe your business goals in this section.

- *Store Appearance:* Describe how your store will look from the front window display, the flooring, to the sign outside. Include merchandise display features, how traffic will flow through the store, as well as the total square footage of your retail space.

- *Unique Features:* What will separate your shop from others? What strengths will your business have over other similar businesses in your community? What previously unfilled product or service area of the industry are you filling? This will also be a part of your marketing section.

- *Management:* In this section describe the store's ownership and explain its legal structure, whether or not you intend to hire employees, and what training you will offer to them.

- *Start-Up Costs:* Lenders are particularly interested in how much you need to get your business running. Provide an overview of your financing requirements, including your own investment contribution, and any additional sources of working capital; explain your business registration, licenses, and insurance. This will be only a summary description. More in-depth descriptions and details about finances will follow in your financial section.

While you should include some details about all of the items above, remember that the business description section provides only an overview. This is to give readers of your business plan a quick summary of how the store will be set up, your starting financial position, and an overview of the management and operation of your store. Some parts will obviously overlap with the more detailed information provided in the other sections.

Legal Structure

The next section to include is how your store will be set up from a legal standpoint. Here you will describe the legal structure of your business, such as sole proprietorship, partnership or corporation. This section may be included with the description of your business, or you can include it under a separate heading. Like other parts of your business plan, you can rearrange the sections or group them together. (You'll learn more about business legal structures in section 3.6.1 a little later in this chapter.)

Location

If you have not already chosen a location, then explain the type of space you wish to lease or purchase, and why you think it is a prime location for your store. If you need help finding a location, contact a local realtor to find out what is available for lease. If you have already chosen a location, then describe it and detail the positive points about where it is situated and why the site will be a good one for your business.

Your Market

Who are your potential customers and why? Use census information (see box below) to show you have done your homework. Include any information on upcoming construction or stores that may be planning to build in the neighborhood. You can get this information from your local zoning board, as new businesses will have to obtain permits from them.

For example, let's say that a complementary business or other facility, one that might bring additional customers into your store, is scheduled to open the week before your store opens. A new daycare facility opening nearby might bring in extra customers for a store offering children's products, or a new movie theatre in the neighborhood might attract an evening clientele for a restaurant; these are examples of complementary businesses. The opening of such a complementary business could potentially bring you a lot of extra customers, just as a new school, new housing development, and many other establishments could provide new customers.

How to Find Information on Your Market

Before opening your store in a particular area, find out if the market is right. For example, if the business you want to open requires a certain demographic (particular population characteristics) and that demographic is under-represented or lacking entirely, or if there are already several store similar to your own in the neighborhood, then you will need to decide if it's worthwhile starting your business in that area.

It is important to research this topic thoroughly. It could be vital to the success of your business. Census reports will help you with general information such as the average age of a city's residents or the number of children in the area. You can locate your area's latest census data at the U.S. Census Bureau website (**www. census.gov**) or Statistics Canada's census pages at **www12.statcan. ca/English/census**.

A visit to your local realty office can also prove worthwhile. Many realty companies keep statistics on the types of families moving into the area. It is also a good idea to talk to your local government (the zoning board is a good place to start) and find out if any permits have been granted for housing or business development. New housing additions often attract young families, whereas condominiums and apartments may be more likely to attract singles to the area.

Another good place to look is on the website of your local municipality. These websites often have employment statistics about local industries, level of education of the populace, and other important economic data. The local Chamber of Commerce can also provide similar information. Another website you can check out is **www.city-data.com**, where you can click on your state then your locality to find basic population and other related data.

Competition

List your competition. While it may not be a good idea to list every single competitor, it is a good idea to list a couple of the toughest ones. This will show the bank or investors you have realistic expectations about your business and are aware of what you need to do to survive. You can find where these stores are located by asking area residents or checking your local Yellow Pages.

Inventory and Pricing

Here, you will explain how you plan to acquire goods. List any suppliers you plan to work with, and what items you will need for the daily operation of your store.

You may have to estimate prices, so your homework on other stores and what they offer and the prices they charge will be invaluable. A good rule of thumb for estimating what you should sell an item for is to price it at double the price of your cost for the item. For example, if you have a product that you purchased for $10.00, then you would sell it for $20.00 (100% markup on purchase, or 50% on selling). You can obtain the latest prices for items from websites and current catalogs.

You should also include what your potential profit on these items will be. Your profit will vary depending on local market demand for your products, sales volumes for a particular product, and wholesale costs. See section 5.3 for more about how to determine retail prices and track profitability for your merchandise.

Marketing

How will you determine your target market and then get the word out about your new business? Be detailed here. List specific marketing campaigns you plan to use; for example, local newspaper ads, flyers, and special signs. (To learn more about marketing see Chapter 6.)

Management and Staff

This section should highlight your background and business experience. This is also a good place to explain your passion for what you will be selling. You are selling yourself in this section. List any type of business background, from working in retail to relevant classes you have taken.

This section also includes information about staffing. It is unlikely you can do all the work yourself. Even if you do not plan to hire others right away, you should have a contingency plan in case you are ill, or some other catastrophe strikes. At the very least, you should make it clear you have several family members or friends willing to step in and help in case of an emergency. If you do plan to hire staff, then state that here, and mention your projected labor costs.

Financial Statements

This is the bottom line that most banks and investors will want to see. This will include start-up budgets, an estimation of revenue and expenses and a projection of when profitability will occur. See section 5.5 for more information on creating financial statements and details about financial planning for your business.

3.4.2   Start-Up Financial Planning

In the next section, you'll find a sample business plan for a new retail store. It includes samples of financial statements, including cash flow and income statements and a balance sheet. Before you look at those, let's examine the basics of financial planning and how it affects the success of your business when you're starting out.

Financial management is crucial to running a successful business. One of the first important questions you should find an answer for is how you will finance your monthly expenses until you turn a profit. These ongoing monthly costs will include things like mortgage, renting or leasing costs; employee wages; utilities, store supplies and so on. In addition, you'll need to decide how much you will pay yourself and your staff, how much you want to save for unexpected expenses, and how much you will put back into the business to finance growth.

When writing your business plan, be realistic. It is better to overestimate costs and underestimate profit. If you make more than expected in your first few months to a year, then so much the better. You will be in great shape!

Budgeting Basics

If you have ever sat down and calculated how much money you'll need for something like the family vacation by figuring out what your income and expenses are, you already know how to budget. The most difficult part of budgeting for a business is that unlike when you work for a steady paycheck, it's more difficult to project your expected income after you pay all your expenses out of your revenues.

To clarify the situation in your business plan you will need to determine, as best you can, both your start-up costs and your operating costs. The start-up budget will include all the costs necessary to get your business up and running. Your operating costs will be all of the ongoing expenses once the business is in operation. In your planning, be clear about where the money is going and why, and explain how you came to your conclusions.

For starters, having a buffer of at least six months' finances available to cover your basic expenses is a good idea, just in case the business does not create a profit immediately. Many businesses will take up to a year to see a profit. Your store may show a profit sooner, but it's best to be prepared.

In the cash flow projections in the sample business plan coming up in the next section, you will see that the company starts out with $35,000 cash on hand. This comes partly from the owner's cash savings and partly from an expected loan. The $35,000 helps to carry the business through at least the first six months as the company finishes this period with an ending cash number of nearly $12,000. Without the cash on hand at the beginning, the company may not have made it through to the end of the first six months. Its total expenses for the period were more than $60,000 including start-up costs. As you can see, that initial boost covered most of the business's monthly expenses for the first half of the year.

Here are some things you should consider when completing your revenue forecast and financial projections:

- Market trends and cycles

- Any seasonality of the business

- Varied sources of revenue

- Holidays (note that in the sample plan, revenues for December were projected as being higher than the months before and after)

- Unexpected events (such as equipment breakdowns, personal illness, etc.)

- How will you monitor your cash flow?

The financial section of your business plan will include your financial projections, break-even analysis, a projected profit and loss statement (also called an income statement), and information about your personal finances.

Remember to include the following items in your budgets. Notice that some expenses overlap on the start-up and operating budgets.

- *Start-up budget:* Legal and professional fees, licenses and permits, equipment, insurance, supplies, marketing costs, accounting expenses, utilities, payroll expenses.

- *Operating budget:* Make a month to month budget for at least your first year of operations, including expenses such as: staff (even if it's only your salary), insurance, rent, loan payments, advertising and promotions, legal and accounting fees, supplies, utilities, dues and subscriptions, fees, taxes and maintenance.

You can get a good idea for the cost of many of these budget items by browsing business supply websites, talking with realtors for rental costs, and basing your wages at minimum hourly wage to start. You may want to pay higher than minimum wage to your staff in order to get more qualified employees. At times, you may have to make an educated guess based upon your research and your chats with other business owners.

List expected profits and/or losses for at least the first year, but preferably for three years. You will want to break this down on a month-to-month basis. Show where the money is going and how much you expect will come in. If the business plan is for a loan, explain how much you need to borrow, why you need that much (exact uses of money), and where you plan to obtain it.

Sample Start-up Budget Amounts

The following is an example of a start-up budget to open a hypothetical bridal salon.

Item	Low	High
Training Expenses	$1,000	$6,000
Real Estate Costs	15,000	30,000
Fixtures	10,000	40,000
Signs	1,500	8,000
Computer Equipment	10,000	15,000
Advertising	1,000	5,000
Inventory, Supplies	20,000	100,000
Loan Fees	1,500	2,500
Incorporation	500	1,000
Licenses, Permits	400	3,000
Supplies, Misc.	3,000	5,000
Working Capital	25,000	40,000
TOTAL:	**$88,900**	**$254,400**

Estimating Your Revenues

Depending on your geographic location, your revenues can be in the tens to the hundreds of thousands. Of course, this amount also varies greatly depending upon the demand for your products, what you pay to your suppliers, and how much you market your business.

Speak with other store owners in your general region of the country but are not competition for you. If you live in Indiana, consult with storeowners in Ohio, Illinois and Kentucky. If you live in California, consult with store owners up the coast, in Oregon or Washington for example. If you live in New York, consult with store owners in New Jersey.

One way to figure out how much you will need to sell to make a profit is to figure out the average cost of your items. (We'll look at how to figure out a break-even point based on your estimated expenses, including inventory, a little later in this section.) Depending on the suppliers you will deal with, you might be able to get a copy of a wholesale catalogue or get access to wholesale prices on the supplier's website. You may have to open a merchant account with them first, though. Once you have done a little research on who your suppliers will be, you can go ahead and contact them to get more information about your initial inventory costs.

Sales Projections

Before you can start your budget, you must arrive at some reasonable monthly sales projections. Many business decisions will be based on the level of sales that you forecast, so if you're too optimistic, you might find your business in trouble. As mentioned earlier, it's always best to be conservative in your estimates.

Alternatively, if you underestimate the amount of sales, you might make decisions that hold back the growth of your business, such as deciding on a less-than-perfect store location because the rent or building purchase price is cheaper. A certain amount of "guesstimating" is required, but you can learn as much as possible about your market beforehand in order to make the estimates more accurate.

There are two types of revenue forecasting methods: Top Down Method and Bottom Up Method.

Top Down

The Top Down Method is what retail operations most frequently use because you can fairly accurately estimate your total market size and from that the amount of money you can reasonably expect to earn from sales.

To use the Top Down Method you must first estimate what the total sales potential would be. This type of information often can be gathered through the Chamber of Commerce, government census data, or from local, state, or national retailers' organizations. Then, by estimating what share of that market you can reasonably expect, you arrive at your possible sales for the year.

Calculation for Top Down Forecasting

Step 1:   Total market size x average annual spending (by customers in businesses like yours) per family or per person = total market potential

Step 2:   Total market potential (from Step 1) x number of competitors = average market share

Step 3:   Average market share (from Step 2) x your estimated percentage of market share = potential annual sales

Bottom Up

The Bottom Up Method is most often used when forecasting revenues from delivering a service. Depending on your business, you might need to use both Top Down and Bottom Up.

The Bottom Up Method is what you will use to calculate revenues from offering services only. Service revenues are limited by the number of hours you can reasonably work. You must first calculate your rate per hour (if you have several services you're offering, use an average price per hour and average production time to make the calculations easier).

Calculation for Bottom Up Forecasting

Step 1:   Hourly rate x number of hours available to work in a day = average daily sales

Step 2: Average daily sales (from Step 1) x number of days you can work per year = possible annual sales

Step 3: Possible annual sales (from Step 2) x expected rate of efficiency = projected annual sales.

NOTE: Rate of efficiency is usually about 50% in the first year. Any guaranteed contracts would have a 100% efficiency rate.

Operating Budgets

The first step in creating an operating budget is to determine what your monthly costs are. Take any bills, such as insurance and taxes, that occur either quarterly or yearly, and divide them by 4 (quarterly) or 12 (yearly) to find out how much you pay for those expenses each month.

Sample Budget Analysis for a Retail Store

Step 1: Data collected for the year projections

Description	Expenses	Revenues
Yearly projected revenue		$112,500
Lease	22,200	
Wages	18,000	
Loan repayments	8,000	
Office expenses	1,400	
Utilities	3,600	
Cost of Goods Sold*	27,900	
Taxes and membership fees	3,000	
Equipment & maintenance	5,000	
Advertising	4,425	
Totals	$93,525	$112,500
Yearly Net Profit = $18,975		

Step 2: Monthly Budget Analysis

Description	Expenses	Revenues
Yearly projected revenue		$9,375
Lease	1,850	
Wages	1,500	
Loan repayments	667	
Office Expenses	117	
Utilities	300	
Cost of Goods Sold*	2,325	
Taxes and membership fees	250	
Equipment & maintenance	417	
Advertising	369	
Totals	$7,795	$9,375
Monthly Net Profit = $1,580		

NOTE: The accounting definition of Cost of Goods Sold (COGS) is: opening inventory + cost of purchases – closing inventory. If you use inventory tracking software, you can get a good idea of your COGS on an ongoing basis, although this is not as accurate as doing regular physical inventory counts.

With these annual and average monthly figures projected, the retail owner can now take a look at where the money is being spent and make some informed decisions about how to cut back on some of the expenditures in order to grow profits. Coming up, we'll show you how to calculate a break-even point for your retail business based on the projections you have already made for your operating expenses.

If you'd like more information about budgeting for your business, check out the article, "Basic Budgets for Profit Planning", on the U.S. Small Business Administration website. The web page address is **www.sba. gov/idc/groups/public/documents/sba_homepage/pub_fm8.pdf**.

TIP: Every month, take a look at your expenditures and your sales, and update your budget and financial statements. A large setback, say purchasing an item that won't sell, or a repair to your vehicle, will mean you must redo your projections and budgets.

Calculating Your Break-even Point

Break-even analysis is a good way to find out how much you must sell in order to cover your costs. (You can compare the result with your projected revenues to see how they match up.) This is without profit or loss; profit comes after the break-even point. Figuring out your break-even point involves a fairly straightforward calculation. You must, however, have all the figures ready in advance before you can get an accurate number. In addition, in order to calculate the break-even point, you'll first need to break out fixed (non-controllable) costs like rent from variable costs like supplies.

Sample Break-Even Point

The formula is:

$$\text{Break-even point} = \text{Total fixed costs}/ (1 - \text{total variable costs/revenues})$$

Using the numbers from the sample budget analysis we did earlier, let's say your store has fixed expenses of $22,200 for lease payments and $8,000 for loan costs (totaling $30,200) during the first year. The rest of the budget expenses are variable costs, totaling $63,325. Based on revenues, variable costs are 56% (or in other words, for every dollar in sales, 56 cents is variable costs). Here's how to calculate your break-even point.

Break-Even Point = Fixed costs $30,200 divided by
(1 minus variable costs $63,325 divided by revenues $112,500)

30,200/(1-63,325/112,500)
30,200/(1-0.56)
30,200/0.44
Break-Even Point = $69,000 (rounded)

The store will have to earn gross revenues of about $69,000 in order to break even. This company is operating at 112500/69000 or 163 % of break-even, meaning it is profitable. With these figures determined, you can now look at ways of reducing your variable costs as well as increasing your revenues to try to widen the gap between gross revenues and your break-even point. It's also a good way to see if your projected revenues are realistic when balanced against known expenses.

When Can You Expect to Turn a Profit?

This varies widely from region to region, store to store, and owner to owner. Most stores break even sometime during the first year. You can reasonably expect to start making profits after that time period.

A lot will also depend on your overhead costs. If you are running an Internet store with low overhead costs, you may turn a profit very quickly. Or if you are running the business out of your home and have no rent, then you may turn a profit more quickly than someone leasing space in a strip mall.

One idea might be to start small with an Internet or home-based store and then move to a larger space as your business grows. This way, you'll see a profit much quicker without the risk involved in investing your own or someone else's money.

3.4.3   A Sample Business Plan

Keep in mind that this is a somewhat simplified business plan. You will need to provide more detailed information in some areas, particularly in the financial section (including financial statements) of your plan.

Sample Business Plan:
Something Old, Something New Bridal Salon

Cover Page

Include the title, your name and contact information:

Something Old, Something New Bridal Salon
Business Plan
Bella Bryden,
1234 Wedding Way
Everville, CA 99999
888-555-1234

Executive Summary

Something Old, Something New Bridal Salon is an exciting new concept in the wedding gown industry. While many bridal salons and gown shops exist, few service our immediate community, and none offer the kind of customer-friendly atmosphere or unique products that Something Old, Something New does. Later in this document you will be able to read about these innovative approaches to wedding wear.

Some of our products and services include re-styled and used wedding gowns, bridesmaids' outfits and flower girl dresses that will appeal to a growing market of environmentally and economically aware brides. We will also offer a limited selection of new gowns made with environmentally responsible materials such as sustainably grown bamboo fiber and organic cotton. Using these products and services as a starting point, the store will continue to add other products and services as driven by the demands of our clientele.

Start-up date for the store has been set for October 1 of this year (due to location availability). We will be located at 1234 Wedding Way, Everville, CA (population 40,000). This location is excellent due to its high traffic volume and ample free parking onsite and on nearby lots. In addition, no other bridal salon is located in this area, despite its high concentration of retail businesses and high draw for shoppers. In addition, we are located across the street from a well-attended junior college, from which we expect to draw at least part of our clientele.

The store will be managed by owner Bella Bryden. Ms. Bryden has 12 years' experience managing a large retail dress store, The Clothing Hangar, in Big City, CA. In addition, she has completed a number of continuing education courses, including courses in entrepreneurship, marketing, bookkeeping and accounting. Assistant manager, Bridie Maida, who has been in retail sales for more than 10 years, will provide additional management experience. The store will hire part-time staff as required and as growth allows.

The store can be operated with a minimum of staff during the week, as Ms. Bryden and Ms. Maida will be on-site to manage, restyle, and maintain the inventory. They anticipate hiring part-time sales staff to assist clients with appointments on weekends, and for at least one day a week during the busy season (January through July) to help with fittings and alterations.

As it is highly computerized, inventory tracking and the creation of a customer database will be simple and effective. We also plan to use Internet tools to manage customer relations such as booking fittings, coordinating bridesmaids' fittings, and alerting customers when their orders are ready.

With only three other bridal salons located in the immediate county area, and none in our planned local community area, we expect to turn a profit within the first year of operations. We estimate that, with the high volume of shoppers and the lack of immediate competition, coupled with our unique business concept, we will capture approximately 10-15% of the local bridal market in the first year. This translates to more than $100,000 in sales.

Both the location and the timing are perfect for starting this type of business in our community. We have identified a lucrative market niche that has gone unfilled before now. No other bridal salon in the area offers the kind of forward-thinking products and services that we do. With the extensive experience and savvy business acumen of its management, Something Old, Something New Bridal Salon will be one of the most profitable retail ventures in the area.

Table of Contents

To be completed last.

Description of the Business

Something Old, Something New Bridal Salon will be a bridal boutique offering a wide range of environmentally responsible bridal gowns, bridesmaids' outfits and flower girl dresses in a hip, fun-filled atmosphere.

We will offer a selection of high-end gowns made with environmentally responsible materials such as organic cotton and sustainably harvested bamboo, as well as organic silk. We will also offer restyled used and vintage wedding dresses and formalwear, which allows our customers to find something utterly unique while still being economically and environmentally responsible.

In addition to a wide variety of wedding wear for brides, bridesmaids and flower girls, our products will include wedding-related items, such as veils, shoes and accessories. Many of our used gowns will be purchased from our customers and from a wide network of thrift and used goods stores, while other inventory will come from wholesale gown suppliers, as required to meet customer demand. Accessories inventory will come from So Pretty Suppliers, and shoes will come from Standard Shoe Wholesalers, as well as directly from customers.

Our goals by the end of the year are to be profitable and to be the leading alternative bridal salon in the community.

The store will be open six days a week (except Mondays), starting on October 1 this year, from 11:00 a.m. to 9:00 p.m. Tuesday through Friday, and 9 a.m. to 5 p.m. on Saturdays and Sundays. It will offer the following unique services for brides not offered by our competitors:

- *Favorite designer notification:* When a dress comes in designed by a designer the bride is interested in, we will notify her.

- *Dress donation program:* If a prospective bride donates any used gown (in suitable condition) to our store, we will offer her a discount on her own wedding gown purchase. We will also donate a portion of our profit from the eventual sale of the donated gown to the Brides For Breast Cancer Foundation.

- *Restyle in style:* Our talented seamstress, Bridie Maida, is able to restyle any dress into a one-of-a-kind work of art through her skilled use of embellishments and couture tailoring.

- *Coffee and juice bar:* Recognizing that our customers will likely be in the store for a few hours, we will offer complimentary coffee, tea, sparkling apple and white grape juice.

- *Comfy chairs and couches:* For the wedding attendants or others accompanying the bride, trying on dresses can make for a long day. We provide a cozy waiting area for them to sit and read bridal magazines while the bride-to-be tries on her choices.

- *A spacious, comfortable dressing room:* Our 200-square-foot dressing room offers two large, private changing areas, plus the Mirror Room, where clients can see themselves from all angles.

The store will be approximately 1,500 to 2,000 square feet in area. Approximately one-fourth of the floor space will be dedicated to the changing rooms and customer lounge. The changing area will be located near the back of the store so that customers will be drawn through the merchandise areas to get there. Approximately 100 square feet will be filled by the coffee and juice bar, which will have a wet counter and refrigeration cabinet as well as a restaurant-style coffee machine.

There will be a small (50 square feet) customer restroom located adjacent to the coffee and juice bar, dividing the dressing room area from the juice bar. A further 100 square feet will be given over to the checkout area. The check-out area will be near the front of the store but located far enough from the front door to prevent customer lineups blocking the entry. This area will include a cash desk, POS system, computer/cash register system, and impulse merchandising areas. A private area at the rear of the store will include a small storage space, staff washroom, and owner's office.

Description of the Industry

The wedding industry, despite current difficult economic times, is holding steady. People will always get married, and women will still want the wedding dress of their dreams, even if it means having to scale back on other aspects of their big day or reduce their honeymoon plans.

According to the U.S. National Center for Health Statistics, one in 64 Americans get married each year. In 2006, there were more than 2.1 million weddings in the United States alone, according to the Association for Wedding Professionals International. Combined spending on these weddings was approximately $86 billion. According to The Wedding Report, brides in 2008 spent an average of $1,266 on their gowns, and a combined total of more than $600 on their veil/headpiece and accessories.

(*Conde Nast Bridal Media and Vows Magazine are real publications used for this example. A real business plan needs real data sources, which you can find online through resources such as the U.S. Census report on Statistics of U.S. Businesses at **www.census.gov/econ/susb** *or through industry magazines and organizational reports. Each industry has its own organization.)*

Business Legal Structure

Limited Liability Corporation (LLC). We have chosen the LLC business legal structure because it allows the freedom of running the business as a sole proprietorship and simplifies tax returns while still protecting personal assets.

(*Note to reader: This may not be the best choice for you. Please read section 3.6.1 on legal structure and consult with a lawyer or other professional, if you are still uncertain.)

Business Location

An 1,800 square foot space located in the Green Tree Shopping Center is currently available for lease. The location has plenty of parking spaces and is visible from State Road 9, a high traffic road in town. The shopping center is across the street from the Everville Community College, where many students are, or will soon be, in our target demographic.

In addition, the location is a former ladies' clothing store, and as such has a number of dress display racks, mannequins and a changing room and restroom already in place.

Target Market

The products and services will be marketed to local families and individuals. There are more than 40,000 people living in the area.

According to U.S. Census statistics, a woman's average age when she first marries is 25 and a man's age is 27. As members of the "Echo Boomer" generation (children of the Baby Boomers generation between the ages of 13 and 30) reach the age of 25 to 27, the number of weddings can be expected to increase. "The number of people turning 27 will grow 30% between 2007 and 2018 as the Echo Boomer generation comes of age," says The American Wedding Study, commissioned by Conde Nast

Bridal Media. As a result, one can expect the market for wedding gowns to grow by a similar amount.

According to *Vows* magazine, brides are willing to drive up to 100 miles to visit a bridal salon. This means that our potential market includes not just Everville, and its population of 40,000 people, but the 100 miles surrounding Everville. This brings our total market to more than 500,000 people. Of those, approximately 10 percent are in our target demographic of people in their twenties and early thirties. That means there are approximately 25,000 women in our target age group in the surrounding 100-mile radius. U.S. census statistics suggest that 1 in 32 women will marry in any given year, which means of the women in our immediate market area, there will be approximately 780 brides each year.

A secondary market is to women who are planning to marry at the popular wedding destination of Honeymoon Beach, which is on the Pacific Ocean exactly 60 miles from our store. Wedding parties travel to the area from around the state to get married on the beach and to enjoy the renowned spa and hotel services there. We anticipate setting up an advertising package to distribute to the hotel and spa guests when they book their ceremony.

We plan to capture at least 30% of this combined market with targeted advertising through web ads with sites like TheKnot.Com and word-of-mouth business. This would equate to approximately 260 gown sales. If growth continues as anticipated, it would mean sales of more than 400 gowns in our second year, and approximately 600 gowns in our third year. With average spending on gowns at a conservative $1,200 per bride, that equates to a gross sales potential of $312,000 in our first year.

Inventory and Pricing

- Starting new inventory will be purchased from Better Bridal, a specialty wholesaler that sells wedding gowns made of sustainable or recycled materials.

- Starting second-hand inventory will be obtained through purchases at thrift stores, flea markets and garage sales.

- Once the store opens, we will solicit some inventory through our Donate Your Gown program, and other used gowns will also be purchased from customers for a flat fee of 25% of the gown's original retail price. Only good condition, quality items will be purchased, and all selections will be made at the owner's discretion.

- New gowns will be sold at the industry-standard 100 percent markup over wholesale, so a gown that costs us $300 will be sold for $600. Used gowns that we purchase will be sold for the same markup, unless they are restyled by our staff. Restyled gowns will be sold for 200% markup, to factor in labor costs of restyling. Therefore a restyled gown that we paid $100 for will be sold for $300.

- Donated gowns will be sold for a flat rate of $100 each, which allows us to make a generous 10% donation of each profit to Brides for Breast Cancer. If a donated gown has been restyled, it will be sold for $100 plus $50 for each hour of time spent on its restyling.

Promotion

We will run advertising in the local newspapers, through direct mail, and community announcement areas such as local cable, bulletin boards, and large signs. We will also develop a website and an email newsletter as cost effective methods of keeping in touch with customers. Database software will help us keep track of customers so we can send them promotional offers and news. In addition, we will hold events like trunk shows, bridesmaid nights, etc., to draw customers into the store.

Competition

While there are several bridal salons in the area offering a selection of new gowns, none offer second-hand or restyled gowns. Our main competition is an outlet of the national chain Big Box Bridal, located in Biggertown, thirty miles from here. We expect our unique merchandise and funky style will draw clients who are looking for something more unique than they might find at a chain store. We've also heard from a number of brides that the service at the Big Box outlet is less than friendly, which means they are not willing to shop there even if the prices are slightly lower.

The other potential competitor is the BigMart department store location in the Biggertown suburbs, as this chain department store has recently begun offering a wedding gown selection at low prices.

Competitor Analysis

Factor		Strength	Weakness	Competitor	Importance to Customer
	Something Old, Something New			*Big Box Bridal Inc.*	
Products	Higher quality	X		A little less	High
Price	Slightly lower price	X		Charges more	High
Quality	High	X		Slightly less	High
Selection	Smaller, more unique	X		Larger, more generic	High
Service	Excellent	X		Poor	Medium
Reliability	Extremely reliable	X		Reliable	High
Stability	Low - if we do not do well, we will eventually close up		X	Very stable and established. This is a real strength of theirs.	Medium
Expertise	Very high	X		High	
Company Reputation	None		X	High	
Location	Prime location with lots of traffic	X		Good location. Little less traffic	Low
Appearance	Professional and neat. Well organized.	X		Same	Medium
Credit Policies	Accept cards, cash or check	X		Same	High
Advertising	Targeted, local advertising planned	X		National ad flyers	Medium
Image	None		X	Okay	Medium

However, our custom work and unique approach to sustainable materials differentiates us significantly from a department store, and our excellent and personalized customer service will be a significant point in our favor.

The other bridal salons are located so far away that they can't be considered competition. Indirect competitors include online wedding gown giants such as Bridal Online. However, these only compete against us in price, as our individualized service and customer-specific fittings can't be found at an online retailer. Their shipping costs can be prohibitive for someone wanting to purchase an affordable dress off the rack. They will not offer local promotional events or the personalized service our brick and mortar store will offer.

Management and Staff

The owner and manager of Something Old, Something New will be Bella Bryden. Bella Bryden has worked in retail fashion sales for many years and has attended many local fashion shows, wedding expos and fashion retailer conventions. Her insider knowledge of how the retail clothing industry works combined with awareness of what brides want and need will create success. She has completed several business courses through her local community college. As a result of this professional development strategy she is aware of the most effective marketing techniques for small businesses and possesses bookkeeping and other necessary skills for small business owners.

Bridie Maida, with more than 10 years' experience in a variety of retail settings, and an associate's degree in fashion design from the Art Institute of Everville, will act as assistant manager and seamstress at a starting wage of $10 per hour. She will work approximately 34 to 40 hours per week. Additional staffing will be provided by local college students hired on a part-time basis. We will particularly target students in the fashion design program, as their knowledge will likely make them better salespeople for our merchandise.

Financial Information

Risks

As with any business venture there are risks associated with opening this retail store. One possibility is that our main competitor, Big Box

Bridal, might decide to include a selection of gowns made from sustainably produced materials in their store. However, we see this as a remote possibility since the economics of producing these kinds of gowns allows for a smaller end profit margin. In addition, the store is unlikely to offer second-hand goods.

Another risk might be that Big Box Bridal might further slash its prices and try to undercut us. Since our prices will be lower than theirs to start with, this may impact us if their profit margins are a bit wider than our own. We cannot afford to take a smaller profit margin. On the other hand, we are also in a higher traffic area than they are and we still expect customers who frequent our business area to prefer shopping with us, especially after they've driven all the way to Big Box Bridal only to discover the lack of personalized service.

We believe that our sales targets are realistic based on our market research, but there is always the possibility that our target sales will not be achieved for the year. We will closely monitor revenues on a daily, weekly and monthly basis to ensure that our sales targets are being reached, and if they are not, we will make every effort to discover why not and correct any issues we discover. Start-up capital will carry the store's expenses through the first six months of operations.

Additional risks that might affect our business include the possibility that our second-hand inventory will not be as readily available after our initial start-up. To counteract this possibility, we have contracted Ms. Maida's sister, a graphic designer in a large metropolitan area in an adjacent state, to source used gowns in her area. She will do this for no charge for the first three years because Ms. Maida has agreed to sew her a custom wedding gown.

[You should include any additional risks that you can think of that might affect your business.]

Cash Flow

Excluding the spike in cash flow for January sales increases, we project positive cash flow beginning in April of next year. Following are our cash flow projections for the first two quarterly periods of operations (note that these figures include sales projections for the first month of operations starting in the second half of September through October 31):

Something Old, Something New Cash Flow Projections: 1st Six Months of Operations

	Oct	Nov	Dec	Jan	Feb	March
Cash on Hand	$35,000	$9,050	$6,450	$3,450	$775	($255)
Sales Revenues	6,000	5,400	4,500	4,725	5,670	6,800
Total Cash and Sales	**41,000**	**14,450**	**10,950**	**8,175**	**6,445**	**6,545**
START-UP EXPENSES						
Construction	$10,000					
Equipment/Supplies	5,000					
Inventory	8,000					
Licenses	500					
Insurance	1,200					
Total Start-up Costs	**24,700**					
ONGOING EXPENSES						
Rent	$800	800	800	800	800	800
Advertising	200	200	200	100	100	100
Accounting	150	150	150	150	150	150
Legal	300	150	150	150	150	150
Telephone	100	100	100	100	100	100
Utilities	250	250	250	250	250	250
Wages	4,000	3,000	3,000	3,000	3,000	3,000
Taxes	800	800	800	800	600	600
Office supplies	200	100	100	100	100	100
Inventory purchases		2,000	1,500	1,500	1,000	1,000
Loan repayment	450	450	450	450	450	450
Total Ongoing Expenses	**7,250**	**8,000**	**7,500**	**7,400**	**6,700**	**6,700**
Total Expenses	**31,950**	**8,000**	**7,500**	**7,400**	**6,700**	**6,700**
Cash Ending	**$9,050**	**$6,450**	**$3,450**	**$775**	**($255)**	**($155)**

[You should create a month by month cash flow projection sheet for the entire year to include in your business plan, rather than the six months in our example.]

Balance Sheet

Following is the balance sheet representing the personal assets and liabilities of Bella Bryden.

Personal Assets & Liabilities of Bella Bryden

ASSETS	
CURRENT ASSETS	
Cash	$10,000
Investments (401K)	$80,000
TOTAL CURRENT ASSETS	**$90,000**
LONG-TERM ASSETS	
Automobile	$12,500
Home Equity	$125,000
TOTAL LONG-term ASSETS	$137,500
TOTAL ASSETS	**$227,550**

LIABILITIES	
CURRENT LIABILITIES	
Car Loan Payment	$400
Mortgage Payment	$650
Utilities and Other Expenses	$750
Property Taxes	$1,500
TOTAL CURRENT LIABILITIES	$3,000
LONG-TERM LIABILITIES	
Car Loan	$9,000
Mortgage	$150,000
TOTAL LONG-term LIABILITIES	$159,000
TOTAL LIABILITIES	**$162,300**

TOTAL NET ASSETS	**$65,200**

[For a start-up company, one without business assets and liabilities, you should create a balance sheet like this to represent the owner(s) total personal assets and liabilities.]

Other Items

In addition to the items listed above, your business plan might include things such as a statement of personal finances (this can include a print-out of your credit history and tax returns), a resume, reference letters, and other items. It is up to you if you want to include these things. Always err on the side of giving more information, especially if you are unsure if you can secure a loan based on the information you're providing to lenders.

Another item you might want to add is a loan proposal or request for funding. In the example financial statements above, the owner will need an additional $25,000 in start-up funding to add to the owner's $10,000 cash in the balance sheet to carry the business through the first six months of operations. A lender or investor will want to see a loan proposal or request for funding detailing how much money you want to borrow, what you plan to spend the money on, and how you plan to pay it back. Under this heading, state the amount of money you are asking for, whether it is a debt or equity funding request (i.e. if you are borrowing money, that is debt funding; if you are asking someone to invest in your business as a shareholder or minority partner, that is equity funding), how you plan to repay a loan, or what an investor gets out of investing in your company. You loan proposal should include:

- How much money you want

- How long it take you to pay it back

- Details of how you plan to spend the money

- How you will get the money to pay back the loan

- A description of your own personal assets and other collateral that you can use to secure the loan

If your business will need start-up financing the next section will tell you how to go about finding it.

3.4.4   Business Plan Resources

You can find a free sample business plan for a bridal salon business at **www.jvbrown.edu/business_plans_handbooks.html#B** (scroll down to the "Bridal Salon Business Plan" link).

Here are some additional resources that you might find useful in helping you to write your business plan:

- *SBA: Write a Business Plan*
  www.sba.gov/smallbusinessplanner/plan/writeabusinessplan/

- *SCORE*
  www.score.org/template_gallery.html

- *Canada Business: Preparing a Business Plan*
  www.bsa.canadabusiness.ca/gol/bsa/site.nsf/en/su04938.html

- *Canada Business: Interactive Business Planner*
  (Free registration required)
  www.canadabusiness.ca/ibp/en/

- *BDC (Canada) Business Plan Template*
  www.bdc.ca/en/business_tools/business_plan/default.htm

TIP: When writing your business plan, pay close attention to spelling and grammar, and try to write clearly and concisely. You don't want to make reading the plan a chore.

3.5 Start-Up Financing

This section covers sources of start-up financing, and what you'll need to present to lenders in order to apply for funding. Additional advice on all aspects of financing your business can be found at the SBA's Small Business Planner website at **www.sba.gov** (under "Start Your Business", click on "Finance Start-Up" then choose "Financing Basics"). In Canada, visit **http://bsa.canadabusiness.ca/gol/bsa/site.nsf/en/su04919.html**.

3.5.1 Getting Prepared

When looking for funding, you must first be well prepared before approaching any potential loan or investment sources. You will need the following things:

- *A Business Plan:* As you learned in the previous section, a business plan is the document that lenders will review to decide whether or not to give you a loan. This document is absolutely necessary for banks or other lenders, and even if you are getting the start-up money you need from a rich aunt, you should prepare your business plan and present it so the person lending you money can see that you have a clear and organized plan. (If you haven't read it already, see section 3.4 for advice on creating a business plan.)

Your financial statements are a particularly important part of your business plan.

- *A Personal Financial Statement:* This should be prepared as part of your business plan. It is important because you need to have a clear picture of your own financial state to know exactly where you are financially before you begin. This financial statement will tell you:

  - How much money you need every month to pay your bills

  - What kind of resources or assets you have

  - What kind of debt you carry. How will you repay this debt while you are putting your total effort into opening your store?

- *A Start-Up Survival Nest Egg:* Many financial consultants think that having a nest egg to live on while you are starting up your store is one of the most important things you can have. Some suggest at least six months' of living expense money — that is, all the money you will need monthly to pay all your personal living expenses, bills, and debts, so you can focus on your new retail business without stress. This is apart from any reserve start-up capital you might need for the business itself.

Asking for Money

Keep these tips in mind when you ask someone for funding:

- Get an introduction or referral. If you can get someone who is respected in the community to introduce you to a potential lender, it gives you credibility and that's a big advantage.

- Have an extra copy of your business plan available for the potential lender's inspection, and be able to speak clearly and concisely about your plans. Be able to discuss all aspects of your business plan, your long-range goals and your prospective market.

- Be professional. Shake hands, speak with confidence and look the person you're talking to in the eye.

- Dress to impress. You're going to be a business owner. Be sure you look the part.

- Be receptive. Even if you don't end up getting any money from a prospective lender or investor, you may be able to get ideas and suggestions from them. Perhaps they'll have some pointers regarding your business plan, or some suggestions about steering your business in a particular direction. Don't be afraid to ask questions, either.

Remember that if someone agrees to loan you money or invest in your business, they're doing so because they believe in you and what you can do. When you ask someone for money, you need to sell yourself and your ideas. Make sure you have a great sales pitch.

There are a number of online resources to help you find out more about financing options for your business. The SBA link noted above is a good place to start in the United States. In the "Start Your Business" section of the Small Business Planner, open the "Finance Start-Up" link and scroll down to find Loan and Funding information. In Canada, you can try Canada Business' "Search for Financing" page at **www.canadabusiness. ca/eic/site/sof-sdf.nsf/eng/Home**.

Now that you know the basics, you are ready to determine who you will approach for your funding.

3.5.2 Equity vs. Debt Financing

In business, there are two basic kinds of financing: equity financing and debt financing. Essentially, equity financing is when you agree to give someone a share in your business in exchange for an agreed amount of investment capital from that person. Debt financing is, as you probably already know, borrowing money at interest that you pay back in installments over time or in a lump sum at a specified future date. (Or repayment could be a combination of these; the point is, you'll pay interest). The decision to choose debt or equity financing usually will be based on your personal financial position and how much additional money you need in order to get your business started.

One form of equity financing is investment capital provided by venture capitalists. You'll want to look for an individual or investment firm that is familiar with your industry. You'll have less explaining of your business concept to do and they might be more open to investing in a company such as yours whose premise they already understand.

While a venture capital investor won't expect you to pay interest and regular monthly installments, they will expect some kind of return on their investment. This could include dividends paid out of your net income, the right to interfere with operations if they think they could do better, or the right to resell their interest to someone else for a higher price than they originally paid for their share of your company. Make sure that you are comfortable with the terms of any investment capital agreement, and that it clearly specifies what your obligations are. Check with a lawyer if you're not sure.

Another form of equity investment comes from your circle of friends and your family. You might be able to get a no-interest loan from a family member or a close friend, with the promise to pay them back at a time in the future when your business is self-sustaining. This is an ideal situation for you so long as the lender has no expectation of "helping" you run your business if you're not comfortable with that. You may also decide to bring in a friend, business acquaintance, or family member as a partner if they have some capital to invest to help cover start-up costs.

Debt financing is any form of borrowing, including a loan, lease, line of credit or other debt instrument on which you must pay interest in order to finance the original principal amount. Sources for this kind of financing include banks, credit unions, credit card companies, suppliers, and so on. If you buy a computer system for your company and pay for it in monthly installments over a couple of years, that is a form of debt financing since you will pay interest on the amount you finance. In the following sections we'll look at some of the sources of each type of financing and the advantages and disadvantages to each.

3.5.3 Borrowing Money

You can choose to utilize any mixture of the financing suggestions that follow. Many new business owners choose a mix of some of their own savings, a family loan, and a small business loan. Only you can decide which financing sources will be the best ones for your business and your personal situation. The most important thing is to make sure you agree to loan repayment terms that you can live with and that are realistic for you.

Commercial Loans

Commercial loans are loans that you can get from a financial institution like a bank or a credit union. You can go to your neighborhood bank around the corner to set up all your small business banking needs, or you can shop around for a bank that will offer you the best loan terms possible.

The terms of your loan will depend upon several things:

- Your credit score

- Your collateral

- Your ability to pay back a loan

There are a number of different loan types you can enter into with these financial institutions. They offer both long-term and short-term loans. For example, you might choose an operating term loan with a repayment period of one year. This will help you finance your start-up costs such as buying equipment and inventory or pay for any renovations you might need to do.

> **TIP:** If you're looking for a long-term loan of less than $50,000 the bank will probably consider it a personal loan. As a result, they will be more interested in your personal credit history, and they may require you to put up personal assets such as real estate as security.

You might also choose a business line of credit if your situation warrants such an arrangement. In this setup, the bank will grant you what is in essence a revolving loan in a specified amount, and will honor any checks you write to pay for your ongoing business expenses. You will pay interest on any amounts outstanding under the line of credit.

Remember that lines of credit are to be used to pay for operating expenses as needed. Don't abuse the privilege by going out and buying thousands of dollars worth of office equipment or a new car for the business. If you do, then you won't be able to meet the projections you gave the lender when you presented the business plan to them. Those projections are why you got the line of credit in the first place.

Operating term loans and lines of credit, particularly if they are unsecured by assets (or other collateral), will have higher rates of interest attached. In some cases, the lender may require that you offer some sort of security for the loan, such as having a co-signer or putting up your personal assets against it. Some lenders may accept inventory (usually at 50% of your cost to purchase it) as a portion of collateral. Another consideration is that your interest rate will change as the bank's interest rates fluctuate.

You might choose a long-term loan, rather than short-term financing, if you need to do major renovations or building, or take out a mortgage if you intend to purchase a building as your retail location. One advantage to this type of financing is that the interest rates are usually lower. This is because the loan is paid back over a longer period of time than an operating term loan or line of credit, and you pay interest at a fixed, instead of a variable, rate. Another reason interest is lower is that the loan is backed by the value of the asset you're purchasing. This makes repayment of the loan more likely. (The lender can always sell an asset like a building if you default on the loan.)

One major disadvantage to a long-term loan is that you will have a debt burden that you will need to carry for a number of years. This can affect your company's growth because you might not have the liquidity you need to pay for expansion or to pursue new lines of merchandise. You might also have to pay a financial penalty if you decide to pay back the loan earlier. Consider all your options carefully before you enter into any kind of long-term debt arrangement. Speak with an accountant and a lawyer first.

Personal Loans

One of the greatest resources for your start-up money will always be the people you know who believe in you and your ideas—your family and friends. Very often they will help you with money when all other resources fail you. They usually will agree to payback terms that aren't as strict as commercial lenders, and they are usually pulling for you, too. As with any other kind of loan, it is important to make sure that you and the other parties completely understand and agree to the terms of the loan. Also, make sure to put everything in writing.

Another possibility is to ask a family member to co-sign a commercial loan for you. Co-signing means that this person agrees to take on the financial responsibility of the loan if you should fail. Family members are often willing to help you out this way. Make sure, before friends or family members help you out by co-signing a loan, that they are really comfortable doing so.

3.5.4   Finding Investors

Venture Capital and Investment Capital Investors

Depending on the type and size of your business, you might consider finding investors to help you with your start-up capital. You find may find that some investors are not willing to invest venture capital in a small, single-location retail store, however, many small retailers have gone on to grow their companies into regional or national chains. So this type of investment may well be something you'll want to look into for the future. As you'll see later in this section, there are ways to find investors willing to put money into small businesses.

Remember that investors are looking to make money by investing their capital in your business. They may or may not be people you know, but they will want you to show them how they will make a profit by helping you. You have to assure them that they will get something out of it, because for them investing in your store isn't personal (like it might be when a family member invests in your business), it is business.

Investors work one of two ways:

- They want to see their initial money returned with a profit

- They want to own part of your business

While investment capital might seem like a great idea, be aware that many entrepreneurs have been burned when venture capital vanished when the start-up money was needed. As mentioned earlier, the investment agreement could contain unsavory terms that give too great a portion of control to the investor instead of leaving it in the hands of the company owner.

However, on the plus side, private investors can be more flexible to deal with than lending institutions like banks. They may not want to get too deeply involved with the day-to-day management of the company. They might also be more willing to accept a higher level of risk than a bank, trusting in your skills and knowledge of the industry and leave your assets unencumbered.

To find venture capital investors beyond your immediate circle of family and friends, you can investigate some of the resources found at the websites listed below.

- *VFinance*
  www.vfinance.com

- *Angel Capital Association Member Directory*
  www.angelcapitalassociation.org/dir_directory/directory.aspx

- *Venture Capital in Canada*
  www.canadabusiness.ca/epic/site/sof-sdf.nsf/en/home

You can also find investment capital through the Small Business Administration's Small Business Investment Company (SBIC) program. While the SBA does not act as an intermediary on behalf of entrepreneurs, they do have a wealth of information about the process of finding investors on their website at the "Small Business Investment Companies" link below.

You can use their services to help you put together a business plan and a request for funding package (see more about this in section 3.5.5), which you can then submit to SBICs that might be interested in providing you with investment capital. You can search for SBICs to match your needs at **www.sba.gov/aboutsba/sbaprograms/inv/inv_directory_sbic.html**.

- *SBA Entrepreneurs Seeking Financing*
  www.sba.gov/aboutsba/sbaprograms/inv/esf/index.html

- *National Association of Investment Companies*
  www.naicvc.com/Home/Members.aspx

- *The National Association of Small Business Investment Companies*
  www.nasbic.org/?page=Find_an_SBIC

You have to decide what you want. Do you feel you will be able to meet the investor's terms? Do you want to share ownership of your business with another person? For some new business owners, the perfect solution is to find a person who wants to partner with them, share the responsibility of their new store, and bring some money to invest.

Partners

One of the simplest forms of equity financing is taking on a partner. Having a partner in your business brings additional skill sets, business contacts and resources to the venture. Most importantly, a partner can bring money to help pay for start-up costs and assist with ongoing operations. You'll need to decide whether your partner will be active in the running of the company or just a silent partner who invests the money, receives income from the business, but has no say in how things are run. (You can read more about Partnerships as a form of business legal structure in section 3.6.1.)

You as an Investor

Never forget that you might be your own best source of funding. One nice thing about using your own money is that you aren't obligated to anyone else or any other organization—it is yours to invest. This can be an excellent solution for individuals with some credit problems. To raise your own capital, you can:

- Cash out stocks, bonds, life insurance, an IRA, RRSP, or other retirement account

- Increase your credit on charge cards (remember that you will pay high interest rates on these)

- Use personal savings

- Take out a second mortgage or home equity loan on your house or other property

- Sell something valuable, like a car, jewelry, real estate, or art

3.5.5   Government Programs

Small Business Administration Loans

The Small Business Administration(SBA) doesn't actually lend you money. However, they have a program called the "7(a) Loan Program" in which they work with banks to provide loan services to small business owners. The SBA guarantees a percentage of the loan that a commercial lender will give you, so that if you default on your payments, the bank will still get back the amount guaranteed by the SBA. Both the bank and the SBA share the risk in lending money to you. As the borrower, you are still responsible for the full amount of the loan.

When you apply for a small business loan, you will actually apply at your local bank. The bank then decides whether they will make the loan internally or use the SBA program. Under this program, the government does not provide any financial contribution, and does not make loans itself.

The SBA also provides a pre-qualification program that assists business start-ups in putting together a viable funding request package for submission to lenders. They will work with you to help you apply for a loan up to a maximum amount of $250,000. Once the loan package has been submitted, studied, and approved by the SBA, they will issue a commitment letter on your behalf that you can submit to lenders for consideration.

In essence, the SBA gives lenders the reassurance that they will pay back the loan if you don't. They provide the extra assurance that many lenders need to get entrepreneurs the financing they need. You can read more about the process at **www.sba.gov** (click on "Services" then on "Financial Assistance").

The SBA also has a "Micro-Loans" program, which offers loans to start-up and newly established businesses through non-profit entities at the local level up to a maximum of $35,000. The average loan is about

$13,000. Interest rates for these small loans vary between about 8 to 13 percent. You can find out more about these loans at the SBA website.

Government Programs in Canada

If you are planning to open a retail business in Canada, you might be interested in the Business Development Bank of Canada (BDC) or the Canada Small Business Financing Program (CSBF). The BDC is a financial institution owned by the federal government that offers consulting and financing services to help get small businesses started. They also have a financing program aimed specifically at women entrepreneurs. You can learn more about the Business Development Bank of Canada (BDC) and its financing resources at **www.bdc.ca**.

The Canada Small Business Financing Program is much like the SBA 7(a) Loan Program mentioned earlier in this section. The maximum amount you can borrow is $250,000, and the funds must be used to purchase real property, leasehold improvements or equipment. The CSBFP works with lenders across the country to offer loans at 3% above the lender's prime lending rate. To find out more, visit **www.ic.gc.ca/eic/site/csbfp-pfpec. nsf/eng/home**.

3.6   Legal Matters

3.6.1   Your Business Legal Structure

Your business structure affects the cost of starting your business, your taxes, and your responsibility for any debts the business incurs. This section will highlight the several different legal forms a business can have. There are four basic structures: sole proprietorship, partnership, corporation (including the S corporation), and limited liability company (LLC).

Sole Proprietorship

If you want to run the business yourself, without incorporating, your business will be known as a "sole proprietorship." This is the least expensive way to start a business. It is also the easiest because it requires less paperwork and you can report your business income on your personal tax return. All you need to do is apply for an occupational business license in the area where your business will be located. Usually, the license doesn't take long to be processed and you can begin operations fairly quickly.

If you're running the business by yourself, your social security number can serve as your tax-payer identification number. If you have employees, you'll need to request a taxpayer identification number from the Internal Revenue Service.

A sole proprietorship means that you have almost total control of the business and all the profits. The only drawback to this type of business is that you are personally liable for any debts of the business.

Advantages

- Easy to start

- Low start-up costs

- Flexible and informal

- Business losses can often be deducted from personal income for tax purposes

Disadvantages

- Unlimited personal liability: the sole proprietor can be held personally responsible for debts and judgments placed against the business. This means that all personal income and assets, not just those of the business, can be seized to recoup losses or pay damages.

- All business income earned must be reported and is taxed as personal income.

- More difficult to raise capital for the business

Sole proprietorships are extremely common and popular among small business owners — mostly because they are easy and cheap to start with the least amount of paperwork.

Partnership

If you want to go into business with someone else, the easiest and least expensive way to do this is by forming a partnership. Legally, you would both be responsible for any debts of the company and you would enter into something called a partnership agreement. There are two types of partnerships: general partnerships and limited partnerships.

A general partnership is when two or more people get together and start a business. They agree on the conduction of the business and how the profits, risks, liabilities and losses will be distributed between them.

> **TIP:** Partnerships don't have to be divided equally between all partners. However, all partners must agree on how the profit, risk, liability and loss will be divided.

A limited partnership is when one or more partners invest in the business, but are not involved in the everyday operations. Limited partners are investors — partners — but they have limited say in the hands-on operations.

Partnerships usually have more financial clout than sole proprietorships — a definite advantage — simply because they have more in the way of assets than a single person. Another advantage to a partnership is, in an ideal situation, you and your partner will balance out each other's strengths and weaknesses. On the other hand, many businesses have gone bad because of an ill fitted partnership.

Below are some of the advantages and disadvantages to partnerships:

Advantages

- More initial equity for start-up costs

- Broader areas of expertise can lead to increased opportunities

- Lower start-up costs than incorporation

- Some tax advantages

Disadvantages

- All partners are equally liable for the other's mistakes with the same liability as a sole proprietorship

- Profits and losses must be shared

- The business must be dissolved and reorganized when a partner leaves

---

Working with a Partner

Beyond any legal issues, before going into business with a partner you should spend many hours talking about how you will work together, including:

- What each of you will be responsible for.

- How you will make decisions on a day-to-day basis.

- What percentage of the business each of you will own.

- How you see the business developing in the future.

- What you expect from each other.

During your discussions you can learn if there are any areas where you need to compromise. You can avoid future misunderstandings by putting the points you have agreed on into your written partnership agreement that covers any possibility you can think of (including if one of you leave the business in the future).

Corporation

Whether you are working alone or with partners, if you want a more formal legal structure for your business, you can incorporate. Incorporation can protect you from personal liability and may make your business appear more professional.

However, it usually costs several hundred dollars and there are many rules and regulations involved with this type of business structure (among other requirements, corporations must file articles of incorporation, hold regular meetings, and keep records of those meetings). Many new business owners consult with an attorney before incorporating.

Here is a list of some of the advantages and disadvantages to incorporating your business.

Advantages

- Protect personal assets and income from liability by separating your business income and assets from your personal.

- Corporations get greater tax breaks and incentives

- Ownership can be sold or transferred if the owner wishes to retire or leave the business

- Banks and other lending institutions tend to have more faith in incorporated businesses so raising capital is easier

Disadvantages

- Increased start-up costs

- Substantial increase in paperwork

- Your business losses cannot be offset against your personal income

- Corporations are more closely regulated

S Corporation

The IRS offers a provision, called an S corporation, where a corporation can be taxed as a sole proprietorship. An S Corporation is similar to the corporation in most ways, but with some tax advantages. The corporation can pass its earnings and profits on as dividends to the shareholder(s).

However, as an employee of the corporation you do have to pay yourself a wage that meets the government's reasonable standards of compensation just as if you were paying someone else to do your job.

Unless you want to wind up paying both a personal income tax and a business tax, you will probably want to create an S corporation. This saves you money because you are taxed at an individual rate instead of a corporate rate.

Limited Liability Company

A Limited Liability Company, or LLC, is a relatively new type of business legal structure in the U.S. It is a combination of a partnership and a corporation, and is considered to have some of the best attributes of both, including limited personal liability.

A limited liability company is legally separate from the person or persons who own it and offers some protections that a partnership does not. Partners in a limited liability company get the same personal financial protection as those in a corporation.

Disadvantages

Regulations regarding limited liability companies vary from area to area. Make sure you do your homework if this interests you. In the end, choosing a business legal structure for your company is a personal choice, and the advantages and disadvantages should be considered thoroughly. Many small business owners begin their independent venture as a sole proprietorship because of the low costs, and incorporate as the business grows and becomes larger and more complex.

For more on business structures take a look at the resources available at FindLaw.com (**http://smallbusiness.findlaw.com/business-structures**). For some additional government resources to help you decide which structure to choose, try the SBA Small Business Planner at **www.sba. gov**. In the "Start Your Business" section, open the "Choose a Structure" link. In Canada, you can find more information about business structures at the Canada Business Services for Entrepreneurs website (**www.canadabusiness.ca**). Click on "English" then on "Starting a Business" and choose the "Forms of Business Organization" Fact Sheet.

3.6.2   Business Licenses

Regardless of what form of legal structure you choose for your business, you'll need to obtain business licenses. This is not a difficult task. All it normally entails is filling out some forms and paying an annual license fee. Contact your city or county clerk's office for more information about registering your business. Contact information can be found in your phone book or online through resources such as the Business. gov website at **www.business.gov/register/licenses-and-permits**.

There may also be a number of other permits and licenses you will need:

- EIN (Employer Identification Number) from the IRS or a BN (Business Number) in Canada. All businesses that have employees need a federal identification number with which to report employee tax withholding information.

- Retail businesses that collect sales tax must be registered with their state's Department of Revenue and get a state identification number. In Canada, you will need to register to collect the Goods and Services Tax (GST), as well as provincial sales tax (except in Alberta), or Harmonized Sales Tax (the HST blends provincial sales tax and GST together in one tax).

- If you are putting up a new building for your store, you will need to ensure you have appropriate permits and comply with any requirements for zoning or access for people with disabilities (see section 4.1.2).

For information about local, state, and federal requirements in the U.S. visit the SBA Small Business Planner (**www.sba.gov**) and choose "Get Licenses and Permits" in the "Start Your Business" section. In Canada, business licenses are issued at the municipal level so check with your local municipality for help with acquiring a business license. For a province-by-province list of Canadian municipalities and their websites, visit the Federation of Canadian Municipalities website at **www.munisource. org/?page=database** (choose "Canada" from the drop-down menu and click "Go"). Many municipalities offer business license applications right on their websites.

3.6.3 Taxes

If you are properly informed and prepared you won't have to face your tax responsibility with a feeling of dread. In fact, once you are organized and you have enlisted the help of a good tax professional, taxes become just another regular business task.

Get Informed First

The best thing you can do to be sure of your personal and business tax obligations is to find the information you need before you start your new store. The Internal Revenue Service (IRS) has a number of informative documents online that you can look at today to learn the basics about everything you need to prepare for your taxes as a small business owner. If you read these documents and understand them, you will have no surprises at tax time.

One helpful document is the Tax Guide for Small Businesses that outlines your rights and responsibilities as a small business owner. It tells you how to file your taxes, and provides an overview of the tax system for small businesses. You can find this document at **www.irs.gov/pub/ irs-pdf/p334.pdf**. For more general information for small business owners from the IRS visit their website at **www.irs.gov/businesses/small/ index.html**.

For Canadian residents, the Canada Revenue Agency also provides basic tax information for new business owners. This includes information about the GST, how to file your taxes, allowable expenses and so on. You can find this information and more helpful documents at **www.cra-arc. gc.ca/tx/bsnss/menu-eng.html**.

It is also important to be informed about your tax obligations on a state and local level. Tax laws and requirements vary on a state-by-state basis and locally, too. Make sure that you find out exactly what you are responsible for in your state and city. In addition, it is important to find out about sales tax in your area.

The Tax Foundation provides information about sales and other taxes on a state-by-state basis. Visit **www.taxfoundation.org** and click on "Data, Charts and Maps" in the left frame menu, and scroll down to the "Sales and Use Taxes" link. The Canada Revenue Agency has a linked directory of government websites at **www.cra-arc.gc.ca/tx/bsnss/prv_ lnks-eng.html** where you can find tax information on a province-by-province basis.

Getting Assistance

If you decide you would prefer a qualified tax professional to help you handle your taxes, you will find you are in good company. Many small business owners decide to have a professional handle their taxes. An accountant can point out deductions you might otherwise miss and save you a lot of money.

One resource that may assist you in choosing an accountant is the article "Finding an Accountant" by Kevin McDonald. It offers helpful advice for finding an accounting professional whose expertise matches your needs. The article is available at **www.bankrate.com/brm/news/advice/19990609c.asp**.

Once you've determined what your accounting needs are you may be able to find a professional accountant at the Accountant Finder website (**www.accountant-finder.com**). This site offers a clickable map of the United States with links to accountants in cities across the country. Alternatively, the Yellow Pages directory for your city is a good place to find listings for accountants.

You will also need to understand payroll taxes if you plan on hiring employees. Each new employee needs to fill out paperwork prior to their first pay check being issued. In the U.S. this will be a W-4 and an I-9 form. In Canada, the employee will have to complete a T-4 and fill out a Canada Pension form.

Both the W-4 and the T-4 are legal documents verifying the tax deductions a new employee has. The amount of tax you will withhold as an employer varies and is based on the required deductions an employee has as specified by the federal government. Make sure you retain the forms in a folder labeled with their name and store them in a readily accessible place such as a filing cabinet in your office.

Check with your state or province's labor office to make sure you are clear about all the forms employees must fill out in order to work for you. The sites below give more information on legal paperwork, including where to get blank copies of the forms your employees will need to fill out.

- *SmartLegalForms.com*
  (Sells employee forms online)
  www.hrlawinfo.com/index.asp

- *GovDocs Employee Records and Personnel Forms*
  (Click on "Employee Records")
  www.hrdocs.com/Posters/hrproducts

- *Canada Revenue Agency*
  (Download the forms you need)
  www.cra-arc.gc.ca/forms

3.6.4   Insurance

Insurance can help protect the investment you make in your company from unforeseen circumstances or disaster. Types of insurance for a retail business include:

Property Insurance

Property insurance protects the contents of your business (e.g. your computer, your merchandise, etc.) in case of fire, theft, or other losses. If you lease space, you may need property insurance only on your own merchandise and equipment if the owner of the building has insurance on the property.

Liability Insurance

This insurance (also known as Errors and Omissions Insurance) protects you against loss if you are sued for alleged negligence. It could pay judgments against you (up to the policy limits) along with any legal fees you incur defending yourself. For example, if the train on a bride's gown is too long and she injures herself by tripping over it, she may consider your product's design to be faulty and dangerous.

> **TIP:** For some small businesses, getting a Business Owner's policy is a good place to start. These policies are designed for small business owners with under one hundred employees and revenue of under one million dollars. These policies combine liability and property insurance together. Small business owners like these policies because of their convenience and affordable premiums. You can find out more about these policies at the Insurance Information Institute (**www.iii.org/commerciallines/whatitdoes/types**).

Car Insurance

Be sure to ask your broker about your auto insurance if you'll be using your personal vehicle on company business.

Business Interruption Insurance

This insurance covers your bills while you are out of operation for a covered loss, such as a fire. This type of insurance covers ongoing expenses such as rent or taxes until your business is running again.

Life and Disability Insurance

If you provide a portion of your family's income, consider life insurance and disability insurance to make certain they are cared for if something happens to you. If you become sick or otherwise disabled for an extended period, your business could be in jeopardy. Disability insurance would provide at least a portion of your income while you're not able to be working.

Health Insurance

If you live in the United States and aren't covered under a spouse's health plan, you'll need to consider your health insurance options. You can compare health insurance quotes at **www.ehealthinsurance.com**, which offers plans from over 180 insurance companies nationwide.

Canadians have most of their health care expenses covered by the Canadian government. For expenses that are not covered (such as dental care, eyeglasses, prescription drugs, etc.) self-employed professionals may get tax benefits from setting up their own private health care plan. Puhl Employee Benefits (**www.puhlemployeebenefits.com**) is an example of the type of financial planning company that can help you set up your own private health care plan.

Association Member Policies

Some insurance companies offer discount pricing for members of particular organizations. When you are looking for organizations to join, whether your local Chamber of Commerce or a national association, check to see if discounted health insurance is one of the member benefits.

Members of the Association for Wedding Professionals International (AFWPI) can get group rates for health (Basic Plus) and dental (Delta Dental) insurance through Capital Association Plans. Premiums and package prices vary depending on your personal circumstances. Visit **www.capsplans.com/afwpi/welcome.htm**.

Members of the Association of Bridal Consultants (including associate vendor members) can get discounted liability and personal health insurance. Again, costs and packages vary. Visit **www.bridalassn.com/mInsurance.aspx** to learn more.

Bridal Association of America members can also get discounts on health, dental and liability insurance. Costs and packages vary. Find out more at **http://bridalassociationofamerica.com/membership/**.

Workers' Compensation Insurance

Another type of insurance to consider if you plan to hire employees is workers' compensation insurance. Most states in the U.S. and provinces in Canada require businesses to have workers' compensation insurance to help protect their employees in case of injury on the job.

To find what workers' compensation laws govern your business in your state check out the U.S. Department of Labor's Office of Workers' Compensation Programs site (**www.dol.gov/esa/owcp/dfec/regs/compliance/wc.htm**). It has links to workers' compensation boards for every state. In Canada you should visit the Association of Workers' Compensation Boards of Canada website where you can find information about the WCB for your province. Visit them at **www.awcbc.org**.

More Information

There are other types of insurance and different levels of coverage available for each type. An insurance broker (check the Yellow Pages) can advise you of your options and shop around for the best rates for you. You might want to check out the SBA's in-depth risk management guide that covers most aspects of insurance planning for small business. You can read it on their website at **www.sba.gov/tools/resourcelibrary/publications/index.html** (click on "Management and Planning Series", then scroll down to #17).

4. Setting up Your Retail Store

Your business plan is written, you have your financing, the legal issues have been dealt with, and all the licenses are in place. You're ready to set up your store. In this chapter, we'll look at the various aspects of putting it all together, from finding a location through how to finish off the interior of your store, to the equipment, supplies and inventory you will need.

4.1 Finding a Location

You have probably heard it before and it's true: location can make or break your store. Finding a space that suits you can take a little work, but once you have the perfect location, the thrill of opening your own retail store will be that much closer! As with any other retail business, the right location is vitally important to the success of a bridal boutique. And of course, what you want is a region of potential customers with a large population of up-and-coming brides, and not too much competition for that market.

To start, you can check with your local courthouse (or agency that issues licenses) to see how many marriage licenses have been issued in your county or region over the past ten years, and whether that number is growing or shrinking. This will give you an indication of the strength of your potential market.

According to recent research and census data, the average bride today is 25 to 27 years old. Check the age demographics of your area, as well as the number of weddings per capita. You can also compare those numbers to a national average to see where your region fits in. The U.S. Census Bureau has demographic and economic data at **http://factfinder. census.gov**.

According to *Vows* magazine, a typical bride is willing to drive two hours from her home to visit a bridal store. That means your target market is anywhere within a 100-mile radius of your boutique location. That also means that all existing bridal stores within a 100-mile radius should be considered competition. That doesn't mean that if your town or region has three other bridal shops, that you don't have a market. What you need to do is look for ways that the existing bridal shops are not meeting the needs of the buyer. Maybe the selection of gowns is limited, too high-end, or too low-end. Maybe their sales staff is pushy, or worse, apathetic. Maybe the prices are outrageous — even dressing rooms that are too small to turn around in can irritate an already stressed-out bride-to-be.

In addition, look for locations near other merchants that brides might visit early in the wedding-planning process, such as popular ceremony sites, reception locations, or jewelry shops. Typically, brides choose their flowers after they choose their gown, and book their photographer later on as well, so locating near a florist or a photographer's studio makes less sense than you might think.

4.1.1 Possible Locations

Traditional Retail Space

Retail space can be found in numerous locations throughout any community. Options for bridal salons include stores in strip malls or buildings on streets with other retail businesses. By locating your business in a strip mall, you can provide convenient parking while setting hours that make sense for your clients. A main street type location has the added advantage of drawing traffic past your store even if they're not headed to another business in the area. In this way, your storefront becomes its own best advertisement.

While shopping malls are also an option that type of traditional retail space is not usually the best choice for most bridal salons because mall hours may not match the time frames during which you want to be open. For example, evenings and weekends are better for many brides and their attendants, and many malls do not keep extended hours. However, the additional parking found around most shopping malls can be an advantage.

While location can mean the difference between success and failure, you also have to consider your budget. How much rent can you afford? Prime locations, especially ones on busy downtown streets or in popular retail centers often have a prime price tag on them as well. You may have to start smaller and work your way up to the store you can afford.

One way to build your business while not spending too much on rent is to begin with a small store, selling only a few limited lines of designer bridal gowns. The location is important, so choose a good location even if it means a smaller shop. Eventually, you'll be able to bring in additional lines or more bridesmaids outfits and move to a bigger space. As your customer base grows, you'll be able to move to a bigger store in a prime location, either near your original store or in a strip mall on one of the main thoroughfares in your town.

Basement or In-Home Store

If you have extra space in an easily accessible basement or another area of your home, you may want to consider starting your store there. This is particularly appropriate if you already have a sewing workshop or room where you design your own dresses. You may find that you can bring clients to your space to see your range of designs, without having to start with outside space at all. You should be able to deduct a portion of your utilities on your taxes but consult with your accountant to be sure.

Operating out of your home raises a number of issues you'll need to consider. For example, you'll need to know if you can legally operate a retail business out of your home (your city's zoning department can advise you), you'll need to arrange for proper liability insurance (covered in section 3.6.4), and you also have residential neighbors to consider.

Many business owners talk to their neighbors before starting a home business. If there is any opposition from neighbors, you can see if there is anything you can do to change their minds, perhaps by keeping particular business hours.

Mall Kiosks

Many malls offer small booths for lease on a short-term basis (you've probably seen them spring up around the holidays to take advantage of the extra consumer purchases during that time of year). However, they can be expensive, depending upon the mall. Smaller privately owned malls will sometimes offer a lower rent for a percentage of your profits. Larger malls are less likely to offer such incentives as they have an easier time leasing the space.

It does not make sense to sell wedding gowns through a mall kiosk, because of the lack of changing areas and mirrors. Also, these do not provide the 1,200-square-foot minimum many experts in the industry recommend. However, mall kiosks are good for selling smaller items such as jewelry, accessories, and other easily purchased and transported items. Consider renting a mall kiosk to sell accessories and jewelry in advance of wedding and prom season.

4.1.2   Points to Consider

You probably have some idea about where you envision your store's location and what sort of a space you are looking for. But to make sure that you don't get stuck with something you are unhappy with, be as definite as possible about all the particulars you are looking for in a space before you begin your search.

As you begin to consider what you need in a space, think about three things:

- Things you must have

- Things you would like to have but can live without

- Things that you definitely want to avoid

Very likely, the first "must have" will be a particular amount of space.

How Much Space Do You Need?

Around 1,000 square feet of floor space is adequate for most retail operations. This gives you enough room to have a good selection and allows one or two people to operate it. However, many new business owners start out in much smaller spaces such as 600-800 square feet. Anything smaller than this and your store will start to feel too cramped for your customers' comfort.

If you have too little space, inventory could end up being crammed into every nook and cranny. Have you ever been in a store where there is no room to move? It is stifling—most customers don't feel comfortable spending much time in stores set up in this manner. However, when they enter a well-organized store that is easy to navigate, they tend to take their time and browse.

About 2,000 square feet is a good size for a store with two full time and two part-time employees.

Space is often costly, though, because many retail property owners charge rent by the square foot. You may wind up having to compromise and, if you do, it can be important to limit your inventory accordingly so you do not "overstuff" your store. (Tips on using space are covered in section 4.2.)

Legal Requirements

Another vital issue is ensuring the space meets all the legal requirements for running your store. Consider the following issues as you begin your search for your new store location.

Permits and Zoning

If you are going to make improvements to your space, you will need to make sure that you check your local city, county, and state regulations and get the proper permits to proceed.

Another thing to ask your potential landlord or your local government's zoning department is whether or not the space you are considering renting is zoned as a retail space.

The difference between zoning and the need for a permit is relatively simple. Zoning indicates where a business is allowed by local law to be set up, while permits designate whether a business can operate or not. (For example, many municipalities allow retail pet shops in areas that are zoned for retail, but one selling prohibited exotic species would never get a permit to operate.)

Many jurisdictions also require new business owners to obtain a Certificate of Occupancy. The requirements vary from area to area but many cities require inspections before issuing the certificate.

Access for People with Disabilities

As part of the Americans with Disabilities Act (you can read about the requirements of this legislation at **www.ada.gov**), businesses are required to provide access for people with disabilities. Similar laws exist in Canada (check with your local municipality).

Accessibility requirements may include:

- Floor aisles wide enough for wheelchairs

- Wheelchair ramps

- Wheelchair elevators if steps are present

- Rails in handicapped restrooms

Make sure to discuss this with any landlord you are considering renting space from.

Other Points to Consider

Here are some additional questions to ask:

- In what part of town would I like to locate my store?

- Are any nearby stores similar enough to my store to be direct competition?

- Are any large discount, or big box retail stores, that would affect my business close to the area where I would like to locate my store?

- Are there other businesses or services nearby that might attract customer traffic to my store (for example, a good location for a children's clothing store might be near schools and daycare centers)

- Have I observed car traffic near my store at different times of the day?

- How much foot traffic does this location get?

In addition to these questions, you should consider the following points when looking for your retail space:

- *Parking:* Make sure the parking is close enough to your shop for customers to carry their goods to their cars. If they need to pay for the parking, can you offer a validation service?

- *Price:* Sure that spot on Main Street is ideal, but how much will you have to sell in order to afford it? Don't put yourself in financial distress right out of the starting gate; be realistic.

- *Projecting costs:* Calculate how much this space will actually cost. Ask about utilities, taxes, any extra fees you might have to pay.

Considering all these issues should help you narrow down the list of places to consider. The checklist below has a longer list of questions to help you assess the places you decide to check out.

Keeping Track of Places You've Seen

As you look at properties for the perfect potential space for your new store, keep track of where you have been, what each potential space looked like, and the positives and negatives of each space.

Consider taking along a digital camera on your space-hunting trips to take a picture of each space's exterior and interior so you can more easily remember details of each location later.

To make the process easier, use the checklist provided below for each of your space hunting excursions. This checklist, along with a picture or two, will help you to be really clear about each potential location you visit so you can make an informed decision.

Finding Your Perfect Space Checklist

Date: _____   **Location:** _____

Pictures

- ❏ Exterior front
- ❏ Interior
- ❏ Notes on pictures

Space Location Checklist

- ❏ Does the space have easy freeway access? Which ones?
- ❏ Does the space have handy public transportation? Where and what?
- ❏ Is the quality of the neighborhood good?
- ❏ What possibly helpful businesses are nearby?
- ❏ What possibly detrimental businesses are nearby?

Exterior Checklist

- ❏ How is the overall appearance of the building exterior? Does it need any obvious work? What?
- ❏ Is the building a storefront location?
- ❏ Is there a garden or parking strip area? Who maintains it?
- ❏ Where is the trash area? Is trash pick up included as part of the lease agreement?
- ❏ Is the tenant responsible for sidewalk maintenance? Shoveling snow? General clean up of trash and debris?

Interior Checklist

- ❑ How is the overall appearance of the building interior? Does it need any obvious work? What?

- ❑ What is the square footage of the space? Is there any room to grow?

- ❑ Are the windows functional? Are there enough windows?

- ❑ Is there adequate light?

- ❑ Are the air conditioning and heating systems shared or private for each tenant?

- ❑ Is the ventilation system shared or private for each tenant?

- ❑ Is the space technology-ready?

- ❑ Will you be able to use your own already existing Internet Service Provider if you have one?

- ❑ Is the space wired for cable modem or DSL?

- ❑ Is the space wired for phone lines? How many?

- ❑ Does the space have private or shared restroom facilities? What is the overall state of the existing restroom facilities? Are they wheelchair accessible?

- ❑ Does the space have hot and cold running water?

- ❑ Are there existing janitorial services and is the cost for this service part of the lease price?

- ❑ Does the space have a workroom or break room?

- ❑ Does the space have a kitchen?

Extra Charges

❑ What services and utilities are included in the lease price?

❑ What services and utilities are provided by the landlord for a fee?

❑ What services and utilities are the responsibility of the tenant?

Shared Tenant Services, Spaces, Costs, Responsibilities

❑ Are there any shared tenant spaces?

❑ Are there any shared tenant responsibilities?

❑ Is there a mandatory tenant association?

❑ Are there any costs that tenants are required to share?

Extra Benefits and Features

❑ Are there any extra benefits or features that make this space especially desirable?

Notes:

_____

_____

_____

_____

_____

_____

_____

_____

4.1.3   Signing Your Lease

Signing a lease for your store space is quite a bit more than putting your signature at the bottom of a legal document. There are a variety of different lease options you can have and a number of things to consider when putting together the details in your lease.

Be sure the following things are clearly stated:

- Who is responsible for what repairs?

- What types of signs can you use? Are there any restrictions on sidewalk sales or signs to draw customers into the store?

- Can you change the colors and décor of the store? (Some malls have very specific rules.)

- Can you make alterations to suit your needs?

- Is there any security?

What to Include in a Lease

Your lease is the legal agreement that makes it clear what each party will do (or won't do). Therefore it is vital that you get everything you expect regarding your store space written into the lease. For example, once you have located a space you really like there still may be a number of improvements that you want to have happen before you move in.

Regular Improvements

Regular improvements are the things that a landlord will do for any prospective tenant — no matter what their business. These are the things that need to be done to prepare the space. Some of the things you should expect (although you should check just to be sure) include:

- Having the space prepared and cleaned by a professional janitorial service

- Painting the interior or exterior of the building as part of normal wear and tear

- Replacing worn bathroom fixtures, mini blinds, or broken fixtures

- Replacing worn or damaged carpet or flooring

Specific Improvements Requests

Specific improvements are the things you want to see done to your space to make it the way you dream it should be. This might include:

- Adding partitions
- Installing a door or a window
- Creating storage or office space
- A break room for employees

In short, these improvements are the things you might hire a contractor to do.

Based on the term of your lease (a longer-term lease makes a landlord more willing to help fund improvements), your landlord will need to agree to the specific improvements that you want to make to the space and all of this will need to be included in the lease agreement. You must determine what the landlord will let you do, what the landlord will fund, what you will need to fund, and who will do the work.

> TIP: If the space you are considering needs too many improvements, maybe you haven't found the right space. Consider looking for a space that fits more of your needs before you commit to a long or complicated improvement plan.

Types of Leases

First you will need to consider the type of lease that will work best for your store. Your lease will most likely fall into one of these categories:

Month-to-Month Lease

A month-to-month lease is the most flexible kind of lease agreement you can have. If you think you might want to get out of your lease quickly, all that is necessary to do so is 30 days notice. Naturally, there is a downside to this sort of a lease. With a month-to-month lease, you aren't locked into a price for a reasonable length of time, plus the landlord can ask you to leave with 30 days notice.

Short-Term Fixed Rate Lease

While a short-term fixed rate lease has all the benefits of a shorter month-to-month lease, it also locks you into a fixed price for the length of the lease. This sort of commitment might be wise if you are truly concerned about giving up your current job to open your store and want a short amount of time to see if it will really work. With a short-term lease, you can add verbiage in the lease to determine what happens after the lease ends. What happens next is up to you and the landlord to negotiate.

Long-Term Lease

A long-term lease is a lease with a term of a year or more. Long-term leases that are for several years or even longer are called "multi-year leases." The best thing about a long-term lease is that once you find a great space, you can stay there for as long as you want.

Negotiating Leases

Be very careful when negotiating a lease. If you commit to paying $1,200 a month for two years, that is nearly $30,000. Try to get the shortest term lease available, especially as you start out. There is a possibility this could backfire and you could lose your space, but finding a new space is a better alternative than owing thousands of dollars on a store that is not thriving.

Some store owners don't realize that a lease document prepared and presented by a potential landlord is a negotiating tool. You certainly don't have to accept the terms of a lease that you are uncomfortable with, and you can negotiate for the things you would like to see either added to or removed from the lease.

The lease written by a landlord is written in the landlord's best interests, not yours, so look for what you feel needs to be changed or amended to make the lease fit your requirements. Remember, the process of signing a lease is a negotiating experience. Both you and your landlord will probably need to bend a little to come up with a document that works well for both of you.

Don't feel pressured into signing a lease as soon as it is handed to you. Plan on taking the document away with you so you can read it carefully, and, if you wish, show it to a qualified attorney for advice. Good advice on leasing, including an article on "Negotiating the Best Commercial Lease Terms" can be found at **www.nolo.com/legal-encyclopedia/index.html** (click on "Business, LLCs, & Corporations" then on "Business Name, Location and Licenses").

Sample Lease with Comments

In the sample lease below, we will point out potential problem areas. Note that the comments are simply suggestions about some matters you may want to consider. These are opinions based on our research, and do not come from a lawyer or a commercial real estate agent. As your own situation is unique, make sure you have a lawyer who is familiar with business leases look over any lease before you sign it.

Opening Section

This lease is made between Big Commercial Landlord, herein after called the Lessor, and Bella Bryden, hereinafter called the Lessee.

This is a pretty standard clause in any contract and simply states who are the parties to the lease agreement. If you are a corporation, then you may want to try to use your corporate name as the Lessee. Sometimes, this clause will include your home address.

Lessee herby offers to lease from Lessor the premises located in the city of Greenfield, in the County of Hancock, in the State of Indiana, described as 197 State Street, Suite C, based upon the terms and conditions as outlined below.

This clause outlines the specific space you are agreeing to lease. Things to watch for would be any mistakes in the address. If it is a building with several store spaces, double check that the suite number is correct. You could wind up leasing more square feet than you wanted or losing a prime location.

1. Term and Rent

Lessee agrees to rent the above premises for a term of two years, commencing September 1, 2008, and terminating on August 31,

2010, or sooner as provided herein at the annual rental of 7,200 dollars ($7,200.00), payable in equal monthly installments of 600 dollars ($600.00) in advance on the first day of each month for that month's rental, during the term of this lease. All payments should be made directly to the Lessor at the address specified in paragraph one.

Some of this information is a little hard to break down, but section 1 basically outlines how much rent you will be paying. Double check that the monthly rent matches the yearly sum. Be sure the day you have agreed to is the day that the rent is due and not sooner. Also, you might want to try to get a shorter term on the lease, if possible. Many landlords will negotiate on this point. Two years is standard.

2. Use

Lessee shall use and occupy the premises for an art gallery operation called Something Old, Something New Bridal Salon. The location shall be used for no other purpose. Lessor represents that the premises may lawfully be used for the purpose stated above.

This simply states what your business will be. The thing to be most cautious of here is making sure that all things are listed. One thing that jumps right out in the above description is that it does not allow for retail sales of other items besides the main retail sector merchandise. You may want to add additional complementary lines of merchandise that aren't directly related to the main retail business you're in. You should ask to have this added before signing the lease.

3. Care and Maintenance of the Premises

Lessee recognizes that the premises are in good repair, unless otherwise indicated herein. Lessee shall, at the Lessee's own expense and at all times, maintain the premises in good and safe order, including plate glass, electrical wiring, plumbing and heating and any other equipment on the premises. Lessee shall return the same at termination of contract, in as good condition as received, normal wear and tear excepted. Lessee shall be responsible for all repairs required, excepting the roof, exterior walls, and structural foundations.

As you can probably see already, there are many potential problems with this clause. You may have a hard time getting a landlord to change some of these requirements. While it is acceptable for them to ask you to fix any problems you may have caused, such as damage to walls, the idea that you are responsible for heating and cooling systems is a bit troublesome. This could run into very costly repairs. In addition, the lease does not state what responsibility the landlord has to fix such problems. Ask that this section be made much more specific, with phrases such as "normal wear and tear" defined explicitly.

In addition, you might want to double check with your insurance company to be sure that if the roof leaks you would be covered under their policy. If not, will you be covered for any loss under the landlord's policy and what is the system for recourse?

4. Alterations

Lessee shall not, without first obtaining written consent of Lessor, make any additions, alterations, or improvements to the premises.

Again, this is way too vague. What is their definition of an addition or alteration? If you put in slat walls to display your merchandise, is that considered a violation of the contract? Ask for some more specifics here. The inability to add display fixtures could really hinder your business. Do not wait until after you have signed the contract to find out you can't create the store you have envisioned because of a clause in the lease agreement.

5. Ordinances and Statutes

Lessee shall comply with all ordinances, statues and requirements of state, federal and local authorities.

This is pretty much a given and you really have no choice but to do this anyway.

6. Subletting

Lessee shall not assign or sublet any portion of this lease or premises without prior written consent of the Lessor, which shall not be unreasonably withheld. Any such assignment or subletting without consent shall be void and may terminate this lease.

This is pretty straightforward and standard.

7. Utilities

All applications and connections for utility services on the stated premises shall be made in the name of the Lessee only, and Lessee shall be solely liable for utility charges as they become due, including charges for gas, water, sewer, electricity, and telephone.

This, too, is standard. It is your responsibility to cover your utilities with most landlords. There are a few who will cover some costs. It depends on the building and the landlord.

8. Entry and Inspections

Lessee will permit Lessor or agents of Lessor to enter the premises during reasonable times and with notice and will permit the Lessor to post "For Lease" signs within ninety (90) days prior to the expiration of this lease.

This is pretty standard, however, try to get a specific statement about what type of notice, how the Lessee will receive the notice and what constitutes reasonable times (i.e. regular business hours). It is also standard to allow them to place "For Lease" signs sixty days prior to the expiration of the contract. This is not a major point, but you may want to request it, if you feel the signs might hinder your business in any way.

9. Indemnification of Lessor

The Lessor will not be held liable for any damage or injury to Lessee, or any other person, or property occurring on the stated premises. Lessee agrees to not hold Lessor liable for any damages regardless of how they are caused.

This section is troubling. What if the Lessor knows there is a structural fault with the building, does not fix it and you or one of your customers are harmed? Get the landlord to strike this clause or have it changed.

10. Insurance

Lessee shall retain public liability and property damage insurance at the Lessee's own cost.

This is standard, and you will want this anyway. Some contracts may go on further and state the exact types of coverage you will need and/or amounts. Some will require proof of insurance.

11. Destruction of Property

Should the premises be destroyed in part or whole, Lessor shall repair the property within sixty (60) days. Lessee shall be entitled to a deduction in rent during the time the repairs are taking place. If there are repairs which cannot be made within sixty (60) days, this lease may be terminated at the request of either party.

You will want this standard clause, as well. If your space is compromised, you want the landlord to repair the defect as quickly as possible. Otherwise, you could lose business indefinitely. If they are not able to make the repairs in a timely manner, you have the option of terminating the lease and moving your store elsewhere.

12. Nonpayment of Rent

If Lessee defaults on regular payment of rent, or defaults on the other conditions herein, Lessor may give Lessee notice of the default and if the Lessee does not cure the default within thirty (30) days, after receiving written notice of the default, Lessor may terminate this lease.

This is pretty simple. If you do not pay your rent, then the landlord reserves the right to ask you to remove your store from the premises. You may want to try to get sixty days instead of thirty but there is not much wiggle room with this clause.

13. Security Deposit

Lessee shall pay a security deposit upon the signing of this lease to Lessor for the sum of 600 dollars ($600.00). Lessor shall keep the full amount of the security deposit available throughout the term of this lease.

Although a security deposit equaling the first month's rent is pretty standard, I would want to see a bit more detail here about how and under what conditions this money will be returned to the Lessee. This is pretty vague and you may wind up not getting your deposit back. Landlords have been known to make up phony repair or cleaning charges so they can keep your deposit.

14. Attorney's Fees

In the event of a suit being brought for recovery of the premises, or for any sum due under the conditions of this contract, the prevailing party shall be entitled to reimbursement of all costs, including but not limited to attorney's fee.

15. Notices

All notices to either party shall be provided in writing at the address listed on this contract.

Both clauses 14 and 15 are standard.

16. Option to Renew

As long as Lessee is not in default of this lease, Lessee shall have the option of renewing the lease for an additional term of twelve (12) months starting upon the expiration of the term of the original lease. All the terms and conditions herein outlined shall apply during the extension. This option can be implemented by giving written notice to the Lessor at least ninety (90) days prior to the expiration.

I would try for sixty days prior on the notice. You may be looking for another place and not quite sure if you are moving out in three months.

17. Entire Agreement

The preceding makes up the entire agreement between the parties and may only be modified by agreement of both parties in writing.

Signed this ___ day of _____, 20__.

_____

Bella Bryden, Lessee

_____

Big Commercial Landlord, Lessor

4.2 Store Design

Once you have chosen your space, you will need to decorate the inside and outside. To help you in this task, you may want to start by choosing a "theme" for your store. Once you have decided on a theme, you can choose your store layout, logo, background music, lighting, and even scents that will pull your store and its theme together.

Will your store be contemporary or old-fashioned? Will it be hip and young, relaxing, or upscale? It is important to choose an atmosphere that will draw customers into your store and reflect the type of merchandise you plan to offer.

Don't forget that displays will need to be updated to maintain your "look," so choose something low maintenance. Many customers prefer well-organized stores to trendy ones where they can't move without bumping into things.

4.2.1 Outside the Store

Remember the external appearance of your store is the first impression potential customers have of your business. It should be neat but eye-catching.

Does it need a fresh coat of paint? If the landlord is responsible for outside paint but does not seem in a hurry to finish the project, offer to paint it yourself for a discount on your rent that month. Let's say the paint costs you $30, and it takes you two hours to paint. You figure your time is worth $20 an hour. You would ask the landlord to grant you a seventy dollar credit on that month's rent (arrange this before you paint). Many landlords will work with you on this because it saves them money and the aggravation of hiring an outside contractor. Your bonus is a fresh coat of paint to hang your new, bright sign upon.

Signage

After your choice of name and location, your choice of signage is probably the most important aspect of creating interest in your location. You will want an eye-catching sign that customers can see from the street. A good sign can actually entice customers into your store. Your signage could mean the difference between bringing foot traffic right to your store or people walking right on by.

Your signs should reflect your style. To create more effective and professional-looking signs you might decide to have a local painter create a wonderful, vintage-looking sign for your storefront. Make sure you can see it from a distance and it shows clearly what your shop is selling.

Your sign should make a statement about your store, have a simple logo, and make the customer want to visit you. If your municipality allows it, you might also put up roadside signs to direct buyers to your store.

Logo

With some of today's inexpensive graphics software, it is possible to create your own simple logo and use it on your sign and other business materials. People will come to associate your store with that logo. There are companies, such as MyLogo.com or LogoYes.com, that you can pay to create a logo for you. MyLogo.com will create a custom designed logo for you for about $100 for a basic package. With LogoYes.com, you design your own logo using their online template that uses standard clip art. They charge about $70 for a logo design or $100 for a logo with 100 business cards.

You could also purchase software that lets you design your logo on your own. There are a number of different programs like Logo Design Studio (**www.summitsoftcorp.com/products/Logo-Design-Studio**), for example, which sell for less than $50. If you decide you want to design your own logo with this type of software, be sure they offer a demo version that you can try out first, so that you know it meets your needs. Most local print shops also offer design services, since they already have the software for it. Keep in mind that, if you have already chosen a theme, your sign and logo can be a good place to tie into that theme again.

Lettering and Fonts

Make sure the letters on your sign are large enough that customers will be able to spot the words from a distance. If your sign will be more than 400 feet from the street front, then you will want to use seven- to ten-inch high letters. If you are located inside a mall, where you will not need to be visible from a street, then you may be able to use lettering between three and a half to seven inches.

Watch the fonts you use for your sign. A fancy script may look nice, but customers might have a difficult time reading the letters. Use both upper and lowercase letters for some variety and to make the sign easier to read. The colors of the sign should contrast with one another — dark and light colors work best (black and white, yellow and navy blue, white and royal blue).

You might find hiring an expert for this particular job worthwhile even though it will cost you a little extra money. Most small towns have stores that create signs for local businesses. Be sure that you get several quotes for your project, as prices can vary widely. Also, do not rule out buying the sign used. You may be able to locate a simple sign without a store name at a store that is going out of business

Be sure to check with your landlord or city zoning board to find out about any ordinances on signs. Some cities have very specific guidelines about height and other requirements, particularly if you're in a heritage area where local history is used as a tourism draw. It's better to check with your municipality before investing a lot of money in a sign you can't use.

Also, most malls have specific requirements for store signs, such as requiring a minimum/maximum letter height, lighted signs, etc. If your location comes with a place to install a sign, you will probably be able to order an appropriate sign with the help of the mall's management. Professional sign companies offer design and manufacturing — check in your local Yellow Pages under the "Signs — Commercial" category. Another option is to order a sign online.

Here are a few companies that specialize in signs for businesses:

- *Capitol Design*
  www.sandblastedsigns.com

- *Spring Valley Signs*
  www.springvalleysigns.com

- *American Sign Carvers*
  www.signcarving.com

- *Custom Hand-Carved Signs by Sally Claus Focht*
  www.customhandcarvedsigns.com

- *Lincoln Sign Company*
  www.lincolnsign.com

4.2.2   Inside the Store

Interior design is really one of the most enjoyable parts of opening your own store. There is nothing like planning and preparing for your store, and then suddenly seeing it ready, in all its glory, just waiting for the first customer to step through the door. Planning your space helps you create an environment that customers will love and enjoy being in.

Creating a space that customers love will encourage them to buy — and to return again. Your layout will depend upon a variety of factors, such as the space available, the shape of that space and the amount of items you have available.

To design the interior space of your store, imagine your store full of customers. What are their needs? What are their expectations? What sort of design elements will help your customers move through your door, enjoy the process of shopping in your store, and have a positive experience purchasing what they want? How can you set up a functional store interior that will help them get what they want and leave, happily anticipating their next return trip?

Customers tend to head to the right when they enter a store. Keep that space open and put special items up front. Think about the possible layouts and how you want the traffic to flow through the store. Be sure to leave plenty of room around the cash register in case you have several customers in the store at once.

How can you utilize wall space? If you have ever been in a clothing store at the mall, you have probably noticed how they use those slatted walls and hang hooks with clothing right on the walls. By utilizing this space, they are able to display a lot more merchandise than if they only used the center of the floor. Think about ways you can use your wall areas most effectively.

Store Layout

As you will see from the sample store layout, it is important that the traffic in your store be able to flow from point A to point B. You can print or photocopy the sample below to create a mock-up of your own retail space to help you with designing a layout that works well for your store.

Sample Store Layout

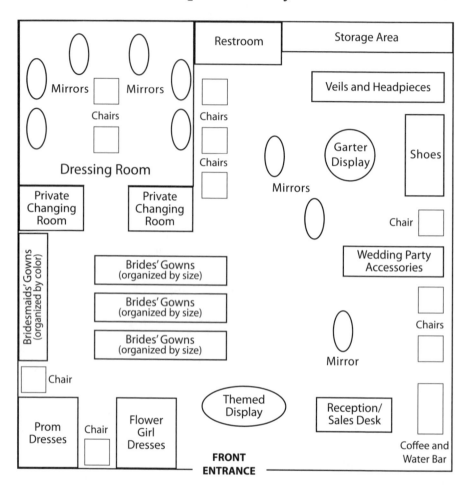

Keep in mind there will be times when more than one person is in your store. If there is a crowd, is there room for them to pass one another? What about wheelchairs or other special needs? The layout of your store can affect how long a customer stays and how many items they purchase.

Have you ever been in a large retail store late at night when they are restocking? Boxes are stacked everywhere and you can't move from one aisle to the next. Sadly, some retail stores don't look much better during restocking times. Do not let your store become a super center nightmare.

Keep aisles clear and easy to move through. Do not shove displays or racks so close to one another that your customers won't be able to make their way between them. Spend some time considering the flow of traffic. Your main aisle should have plenty of room and be easily accessible from the front entrance. Mark everything clearly with signs so that customers can quickly locate items of interest to them.

Your entry should be open and inviting. Have a mat for the entryway and leave space for deliveries. The sales floor should be uncluttered and clearly organized. It should be clear to customers where various items are located. You can use in-store signs that show customers where to find different categories of merchandise.

If your type of business allows for it, an area for children to play can be a good idea. A play area to keep children occupied is greatly appreciated by shoppers with small children. If there is a play area where parents can keep an eye on the children but still have a little freedom to shop, they will be much more likely to linger in your store and buy more. Is your clientele likely to have children? If so, then you will definitely want a small table and some coloring supplies. Some store owners offer small televisions and appropriate videos in the play area as well.

Cash Register Area

Make your cash desk appealing and functional. Your cash register should be in a spot where you can greet customers as they come into the store, while allowing you to keep an eye on the rest of the store. Do not overcrowd the checkout area. Keep in mind your customers may have their arms loaded with items and will want a place to set them down. You should have a worktop that allows enough room for placing purchases and also some business cards nicely displayed along with comment cards, leaving room for impulse displays.

Have you ever grabbed an item you hadn't planned to purchase while waiting in a checkout line? This is called impulse buying, and you want your customers to do this in your store, too. Place interesting items near the register, especially smaller, lower-priced items that people might find attractive or that complement other higher priced merchandise. You might even consider selling magazines, books, or other informational materials. Whatever you do display though, keep it tidy and relevant. You'll learn more about merchandise displays in section 4.3.

Be sure to put out some business cards and brochures for customers to take and share with others. Magnetized business cards are a good investment and remind customers of your store each time they go to their refrigerator.

Another consideration is all the point-of-sale and other equipment and retail supplies you will need at your cash desk. Make sure there is space behind your counter for credit card processing machines, your computer, bags, packing materials and other sales aids. Your cash desk will likely need to have shelving and drawers built into it for storage of supplies.

Indoor Lighting

Harsh fluorescent lighting may sound like something you would worry over in an office building, but it can change the look of items you are trying to sell, too. It can make items looks washed out or a different or unappealing color.

Certain types of lighting can also disturb customers and cause them to leave the store sooner than you would like. If you have ever walked into a bookstore with flickering fluorescent lights and tried to read the back cover of a book, you know how irritating this can be. You don't want your customers walking out on you because you chose the wrong lighting.

Be aware of small things like this. You can become so used to them that you are not even aware of the problem. Watch your customers. Be aware of their reactions and ask questions if they seem irritated.

4.2.3   Store Security

One of the facts of life in retail is that you can become the target of shoplifters. How you lay out your store is an important component of deterring shoplifting. You need to deter burglars as well and your business insurance policy might require you to install an alarm system. A good alarm system can pay for itself in reduced rates and thwarting would-be thieves.

There are many security companies who can provide you with the equipment and support you'll need to keep your store secure. Check out your local Yellow Pages to find security companies in your area. To learn more about security for your store you can check out ADT Security Services (**www.adt.com/small_business**) who offer a variety of services for surveillance and alarms systems for small business owners. Broadview Security is another trusted name in security systems. You can find out about the many services they offer for small businesses at **www.broadviewsecurity-business.com**.

> **TIP:** Check with your landlord to see if they will cover the cost of installation if the alarms are not already provided (you can purchase basic alarms at any hardware or department store).

Not only should you consider having a security system installed, but you need to learn and teach any staff you hire about how to be on the lookout for suspicious behavior. Place a security mirror to reflect corners you can't see from your cash desk. A security camera is also a great idea to aid in apprehending anyone you think might be shoplifting.

To deter shoplifters try not to stack items too high in the center of your store. Keep displays low enough that you and your staff can see over them. Another good tip is not to keep small items in areas where you have difficulty keeping an eye on them.

Ways to Spot a Potential Shoplifter

- Carries a slightly open umbrella (especially if there isn't a cloud in the sky) to use to drop or push small items into, as they "browse."

- Wears a coat too heavy for the season

- Two shoppers come in and one distracts you while the other goes to a hard-to-see area of the store.

- A single shopper comes in and sends the only clerk to the back of the store to find something.

- A group of shoppers comes in and they all separate making it difficult to watch them all.

- Carefully watch customers who are carrying bags, large open purses, or have an arm in a sling.

- Be suspicious of customers who seem to be walking funny, tugging at their sleeves, or holding their coats closed.

- Shoplifters often engage clerks in describing items, but don't appear to be interested in the answers.

- Often, shoplifters will quickly scope the store. Real shoppers tend to seem genuinely interested and less erratic.

- Be wary of people who drop things; this might be a ruse to hide an item.

4.3 Displaying Merchandise

While there are many different theories on how a store should be merchandised, the most important thing is to arrange your items to give an organized and clean appearance.

> TIP: Books and magazines about interior design may give you ideas for displays and help you create a style for your shop. Additionally, most community colleges offer night classes in decorating that would help you understand the principles needed to create eye-catching and pleasing displays.

4.3.1 Maximizing Sales

Where to Place Items

Merchandise with the highest margin of profit should be placed at the front of your store. This way the customer passes it twice—once on the way in, and once on the way out. You want these to jump out and grab customers as they walk in the door and as they walk out. Display these goods in special ways so that they attract attention quickly.

Popular items that most people are looking for (whatever the current trend is) should be placed at the back of the store. That way, people will need to walk through almost your entire inventory in order to get to those pieces. This is exactly why milk is always at the back of the supermarket.

Most stores place their clearance racks in the back of the store. This is a good idea because your profit margin is much smaller on these items. This is not where you want your customers to fall in love with the items they just have to have. Instead, you want them to browse through the main selections first (which will bring you more of a profit), and get through to the clearance racks last. If they spend all their money on clearance merchandise you have at the front of the store, they will not have any left for your high profit items.

Impulse Displays

Think about the check-out area of your favorite big name stores. "Oh, yes," you say as you stand there waiting for the cashier, "I really need batteries, a book light, and some air freshener." This is called impulse displaying and you can do the same thing. Think about placing some special groups of items that people might overlook normally, such as small items or novelty items. You could move any number of smaller items closer to your cash area, or perhaps items that tweak your customers' interest and trigger an impulse purchase. Try displaying different items week by week to see what sells best.

Also try not to stuff too much merchandise onto a display rack. This is an occupational hazard. It is better to leave some items in the back room and pull them out a little at a time than to have racks so full the customer can't see what you have in stock.

Displaying on the Sidewalk

This is a tough one. While you should not put your cheapest things out front, there is something to be said for enticing customers to visit the store. You might build customer loyalty and get repeat customers. A sidewalk store is the perfect way to accomplish this.

Make sure you are allowed to have items on the sidewalk. Read your lease carefully. Some malls (even strip malls) will not allow this.

So, should you sidewalk display or not? The final decision is up to you, but you should at least try sidewalk displays to see if they improve your sales. For example, you could have a sidewalk sale on your high profit items with 10% off (you still make a good profit but still offer a sale). Many merchant associations, especially in downtown areas, regularly host sidewalk sales to encourage shoppers who normally would only visit the local mall to shop in their area.

The effectiveness of this type of promotion may also depend upon the type of items you are selling and the area where you are located. You may want to test the waters. One weekend have your discounted clearance items on the sidewalk and the next keep them inside. Compare the sales for each weekend (they need to be comparable weekends and not when a special event is in town or on a holiday weekend).

4.3.2 Creating Window Displays

If you are fortunate to have a great window with a view to a well-traveled sidewalk, be sure to take advantage of it to make your shop irresistible to passing customers. Think of creating little vignettes with similar items. Whatever you do put in the window, make sure that it won't be ruined by exposure to sunlight.

Window displays are a good place to let your creativity shine. You'll want to put your best items on display. Your goal is to draw customers into your store to view your merchandise. Be prepared to sell the displays and replace the items in the window, though. That's the whole point of the display, after all.

Exciting window displays will encourage customers to come in and browse. Some things to remember:

- Make sure the glass is clean with no streaks. You may have to clean the windows often, particularly if your clientele includes children, but it will be worth the effort.

- Even when you aren't open, you may want to light the window displays to attract new customers who will see the items and come back during regular business hours.

- A few props can go a long way. Think thematically, and try to incorporate things like holidays, special local events or the passing seasons into your displays.

Here's a list of basic ideas to tie in the season with merchandise in your window display (let loose your creativity and imagination from there):

Autumn: Brightly colored leaves and a few large branches with a couple of large pumpkins in the center.

Spring: Flowers and greenery suggest spring. A strategically placed fan can create the impression of a breeze.

Summer: A beach or honeymoon theme is easy with some inexpensive sand, sea shells, and beach balls. (The sand cleans up easily with a shop vacuum.)

Winter: Christmas trees and lights create an eye-catching display. Create a snowy scene using cotton batting or even a white sheet.

Window Design Basics

There are a few design basics to keep in mind when you are designing a window display.

- You should have one item that is your focal point.

- Arranging odd numbers of items on various levels is more pleasing.

- Group items in threes, fives, and sevens.

- Use boxes under lovely fabrics to create more levels, or better yet, a variety of stands, small tables and chairs.

Remember that you need to be prepared to sell items out of your window displays. When you do, you'll have to think of new items to add to the mix that will work as well or perhaps redesign the display a little to incorporate something new into it.

Here's an example of a simple but effective window display for a Christmas theme.

Christmas weddings let your bridal gowns sparkle and glitter like new-fallen snow, so first fill the bottom of the window area with a snow-like substance. You can use cotton sprinkled with glitter, or get sheets of polyester film (such as Mylar) from a craft store and crunch them up to look like ice.

Hang a rich-looking fabric backdrop—a large plain piece of black, deep red or dark green velvet is perfect.

Next, dress your best mannequin in a seasonally appropriate white bridal gown. Try to choose one with lots of sparkle to go with the snow. Maybe add a white velvet stole to add to the look, or an artificial bouquet made with holiday evergreens. Place the mannequin just to the left of the center of the window (as the viewer from the outside would see it), facing her towards the center of the window so she's at a slight angle.

Dress another mannequin in a complementary bridesmaid gown— maybe something in red or green taffeta or satin—and place her on a riser or pedestal just to the right of center, so she appears to be slightly behind the bridal mannequin. Give her a simple bough of evergreen to hold.

Finally, in addition to your regular window lighting, which should be focused mainly on the bridal gown, you can add to this display with Christmas lights. Outline the window with strings of white lights or add a small Christmas tree behind and to the left of the bridal mannequin. Don't decorate the tree with anything other than lights—you want the viewer to be able to focus on the gowns.

4.4 Retail Equipment and Supplies

4.4.1 Items You'll Need

In addition to the fixtures you'll need to display merchandise, there are a variety of other items you will need to equip your store. This section begins with suggestions for various areas of the store, followed by information about suppliers. Check what your store already has, or what your landlord provides, and make your shopping list.

In addition to the items below, section 5.2 has advice on computer equipment and supplies. For information about how to find manufacturers and wholesalers who can supply you with inventory for your store, see section 4.5.

Special Equipment

Mannequins   These are human-shaped forms that model your merchandise. They come in a variety of types, including realistic, abstract, headless, half-body and full-body, and a variety of sizes, including child, junior and adult. You can also buy partial mannequins that model specific body parts like stockings, gloves and hats. Mannequins usually come with stands to help them stay upright. A full-body adult mannequin will cost between $300 and $1,000, depending on style and quality.

Garment racks   Garment racks give you a place to hang all your in-stock or sample gowns. They may be long racks that let you arrange gowns in rows, or circular displays that let you create "islands" on the store's sales floor. Expect to pay between $50 and $1,000 for your racks, depending on size, style and material (metal or wood).

Garment stands   Stand-alone stands that let you display a single garment not on a mannequin. Cost $20-$50 each.

Millinery racks   These spinning or fixed wire racks give you a place to display hats and veils. Cost $15-$50 each.

Mirrors   Floor-length gowns require floor-length mirrors. You can buy plain mirrors to attach to the walls, or stand-alone mirrors to place throughout your salon and dressing room. You'll also need smaller stand mirrors to use on sales counters for jewelry, tiaras and hats, and hand mirrors to let customers see the backs of their heads. Prices vary widely depending on size and trim; expect to pay $10 to $50 for hand mirrors, $20 to $100 for stand mirrors, and $50 to $500 for full-length mirrors.

Shoe displays   Display shoes on wire or Lucite (clear plastic) racks and stands. Expect to pay about $2 for each single-shoe Lucite stand, or up to $80 for a tall stand capable of holding several pairs.

Steamer   It's helpful to have a garment steamer to get wrinkles out of gowns. Expect to pay about $300 for a professional quality steamer.

Selling Supplies

- ❏ Bags
- ❏ Garment bags
- ❏ Boxes
- ❏ Blank gift certificates
- ❏ Signs ("Sale", "Open/Closed", "Store Hours", etc.)
- ❏ Cash register
- ❏ Credit card machines
- ❏ Office Supplies
- ❏ Filing cabinets
- ❏ Desks
- ❏ Chairs
- ❏ Office supplies (pens, paper, stapler, scissors, tape, markers, clips, etc.)
- ❏ Phones
- ❏ Answering machine or voice mail
- ❏ Internet connection
- ❏ Computer
- ❏ Software
- ❏ Printer (consider a combination fax/printer/copier/scanner)
- ❏ FAX machine
- ❏ Copier (optional)

TIP: If you watch closely, you can sometimes catch free or almost free telephones after rebate. OfficeMax, Office Depot, and Staples have all offered these at one time or another. Watch your Sunday circulars and you may be able to find a great deal on some of the items you will need.

Price Labels

Most retail stores use either simple labels with neat, handwritten prices or printed price stickers from a pricing gun or computer printer. If you're starting out on a shoestring budget, you might consider self-adhesive labels, but be very careful. Some labels leave glue residue on items, and will sometimes cause a permanent mark when removed.

Many retailers use string tags that they can tie onto their merchandise. Use these for larger, more visible items because some people might be tempted to remove a higher price tag and replace it with a lower price one from other items. You might be aware of the price of items in your store, but your part-time staff might not.

Some store owners use bar code tags that work with whatever type of software and scanner they are using. It sounds expensive, and initially it might be, but if you get very busy the time you save keeping track of your inventory might pay for it. (You can read more about inventory systems, pricing and labels in section 5.2)

TIP: Worn tags make customers aware that an item has been around for a long time. When you're dusting, take the time to replace worn tags.

Overall Store

❑   Paint

❑   Wallpaper

❑   Window treatments (e.g. blinds)

❑   Wall decorations

❑   Carpeting or area rugs

❑ Trash cans and trash bags

❑ Broom and dust pan

❑ Mop

❑ Vacuum cleaner

❑ Cleaning supplies

❑ Air filters

❑ Light bulbs

❑ Fire extinguishers

❑ Fire alarm

❑ Burglar alarm

❑ Break Room

❑ Tables

❑ Chairs

❑ Refrigerator

❑ Microwave

❑ Time clock

❑ Trashcans

❑ Bulletin board for employee laws and other postings

❑ Coffee maker and coffee supplies

Stationery

If you plan on sending out mailings to clients or suppliers, you may wish to consider having your own stationery printed up. This can include business cards, letterhead, envelopes, and any other special items you can think of. Section 6.1.2 provides detailed information about stationery and suppliers.

4.4.2   Suppliers

Many suppliers can be found simply by checking your local Yellow Pages. However, we have included some links in this guide to help you with your search for suppliers. Office supplies and equipment are readily available and office supply chains offer competitive prices.

General Business Supplies

Office supplies are easy to find and can be purchased at a variety of locations. Office supply chain stores are competitively priced, and may deliver if you buy in quantity.

- *Office Depot*
  www.officedepot.com

- *OfficeMax*
  www.officemax.com

- *Staples*
  www.staples.com

Retail Supplies

To find supplies for retail (such as bags, gift certificates, etc.) you can check the Yellow Pages or do an online search for retail supplies. Here are a few suppliers to get you started. You may need a copy of your retail license to get the wholesale rate or to avoid paying sales tax.

- *NEBS*
  www.nebs.com

- *Paper Mart*
  www.papermart.com

- *Bags & Bows*
  www.bagsandbowsonline.com

- *Store Supply Warehouse*
  www.storesupply.com

- *Motorola Retail Solutions*
  www.symbol.com/retail

- *POS World*
  www.posworld.com

Supplies for Bridal Salons

Here are some examples of companies that provide supplies especially for bridal salons:

- *Vaudeville Mannequins*
  (Shipping cost is about $100 in the U.S. and Canada. Click on "Contact Us" for more information.)
  www.vaudevillemannequins.com

- *Mannequin Madness*
  (Sells used mannequins and forms.)
  www.mannequinmadness.com

- *Robert H. Ham (display racks, store fixtures)*
  www.robertham.com

Cash Registers

You will need a safe place to keep your cash. You may decide to use a common lockbox, or you may want something more advanced. You can purchase cash registers that can be programmed to work with your computer or you can purchase freestanding systems. You may want to start simple and then upgrade to a deluxe model as your business grows.

As with other types of equipment, there are a number of places you can find cash registers (including eBay) for used and your local office supply store or cash register supplier for new.

- *eBay*
  www.ebay.com

- *Cash Register Store*
  http://cashregisterstore.com

- *Cash Register Sales, Service and Supply, Inc.*
  www.cashregisterman.com

Display Fixtures

To find shelves and fixtures for displaying the merchandise you are selling, you can check the Yellow Pages or do an online search for retail fixtures. The Yahoo! Business Directory at **http://dir.yahoo.com/ Business_and_Economy** lists a large number of companies that sell store fixtures. To find these, choose the "Business to Business" link and then scroll down to the "Retail Management" link, where you'll find a "Fixtures" link.

Here are a few additional sites to get you started:

- *Display Warehouse*
  www.displaywarehouse.com

- *Franklin Fixtures*
  www.franklinfixtures.com

- *Victory Display Equipment*
  www.victorydisplay.com

- *Eddies*
  www.eddies.com

You might also consider building the fixtures yourself or hiring someone to do so. For used displays, try publications like The Trader (**www. traderonline.com**), and check out the classifieds in your local newspaper. Do not overlook auction sites like eBay for additional opportunities to pick up display racks at a reasonable price. Also be on the lookout for stores going out of business. You can approach them and offer to purchase their display fixtures.

4.5 Your Bridal Salon Inventory

"Research, research, research replaces Location, location, location. You have to stay up on trends and think ahead about what will be popular next year or you will be stuck with dresses that do not sell."

— Haley Hughes, En Vogue Events, Houston, TX

Without a doubt, the most important items you will purchase for your retail store are the products you will sell. The online encyclopedia, Wikipedia, defines inventory as "a list of goods and materials held available in stock that also brings associated costs for space, for utilities, and for insurance to cover staff to handle and protect it." These are important concepts to keep in mind when purchasing your inventory.

You'll want to match your inventory to your clientele and make sure that you know how to choose the right products as well as where to find them. You don't want your inventory collecting dust in your store and tying up your valuable space and resources.

However, there's value to being a little bit different. As Lillie Garrido, of White Couture Designer Bridal and Tuxedos, Park City, UT, says, "Go outside of the box and offer a unique variety. Even if you only sell the popular look, the unique look drives the customer in the door because they are all curious to try it on. They may buy the safe gown but at least you made the sale."

4.5.1   Building Your Inventory

How much do you need at first? That is a personal preference. Some retail store owners want to have a large quantity of items before opening, and others only need a few items to get started. Below are some tips to help you develop a starting inventory and where you can find merchandise to sell.

To develop your inventory, you'll need to order a selection of gowns from wholesalers. Not only will you need to have a variety of styles for your customers to choose from, but you'll need a range of sizes for them to try on. How much inventory you carry will depend on what start-up cash you have available, and the size of bridal salon you plan to open.

Remember, when you buy gowns from wholesalers, you're usually buying samples. Your customers can try these dresses on and, if they choose to buy, have one made especially for them by the manufacturer to ensure a custom fit. It's important to note that many of the top wedding gown manufacturers require you to buy a minimum number of samples per season (twice a year). Minimums can range from 4 to 20 samples per season.

This may not seem like much, but it can add up. For example, if you are ordering 20 dresses at a cost of $500 each from only four designers, this could mean a required output of $40,000 twice a year just on samples from these four designers. Stocking eight designers will cost you $160,000 a year.

In order to get around this buying minimum and still carry a decent variety of designers, local bridal boutiques have been known to partner up into buying networks and pool their buying to meet the minimums. This is where networking with other bridal salon owners will help you. (See section 6.2.4 for more about networking and section 2.4.1 for tips on finding other bridal salon owners.)

Another option would be to become an authorized dealer of only a few lines, where you carry the full range of gowns from a handful of select dealers. In this case you will want to strongly believe in the designers, as their creativity and vision will make or break the success of your boutique.

4.5.2 Inventory Purchasing Considerations

When you have browsed bridal magazines and websites and decided what designers most appeal to you, you can contact the manufacturers directly to inquire about carrying their lines. Most of the designers' websites have contact information for retailers, and will put you in touch with a sales rep.

The major bridal trade show where the latest and greatest styles are put on display and you can place orders for the upcoming season is the National Bridal Market, held twice a year (spring and fall) in Chicago. Like most fashion trade shows it is open to retail buyers only (not the general public). Even if you don't plan to buy, you can get a sense of what will be in style in the upcoming months. Visit the website at **http://nationalbridalmarket.com** to find out upcoming dates for this major event. You can access a list of many of the popular bridal gown manufacturers at The Knot's wedding gown designer list at **http://weddings.theknot.com/weddingdress/bs_main.aspx**. (You'll need to register for a free membership before you can view the dresses.)

For every bridal line you carry, you'll want to order a range of sizes to accommodate your clientele. The most popular bridal sizes are 10 and

12 (these will generally fit a woman who usually wears a size 8 or 10). You can also carry 8s and 14s if you have the money and the space.

Experts recommend, if you have only a few sample sizes of each style, to err on the side of larger sizes. It's easier to take in a larger gown to make it fit, than to force a larger client to imagine how a smaller gown will look on her.

Carefully consider which gowns you want to carry. There are hundreds of great designers, but you will have to be selective. There are varied price points as well, so match your gowns to what you envision your customers to want.

> *"Because of the mark-up price on the gown you can easily do promotions with discounts. Don't give up; if something isn't selling don't buy more of it but try to re-market it. Light it up differently. You may create a must-have piece."*
>
> — Haley Hughes, En Vogue Events, Houston, TX

TIP: You can sell your old samples as off-the-rack gowns. Try marking them down by 20 or 30 percent off the suggested retail price. You'll still make a small profit, and clear out dresses that would otherwise take up valuable room in your store. A sample sale is an especially good way to clear out bridesmaid dresses, especially in the months before prom or the holiday party season.

4.5.3   Who to Buy From

Wholesalers

A wholesaler buys products from the manufacturer, usually in large quantities, and resells them in smaller lots to retailers. As a result, the wholesaler is sometimes referred to as the "middleman" between retailers and manufacturers. Wholesalers can include companies that sell gowns, accessories, or other wedding-related products.

You can also find wholesalers in the Yellow Pages under whichever category you are looking for. Another option is to check directories at your local public or university library. Look for the American Wholesalers and Distributors Directory from the publisher (Gale); chances are you can find this or similar directories at the library.

Manufacturers and Designers

You will get the best deal if you can buy directly from the manufacturer or designer. However, some may not be willing to sell to you because of their arrangements with their current wholesalers. In those cases, you will need to go to the wholesaler.

Designers are companies that make products, usually in larger quantities. Many designers sell to wholesalers, and will not sell directly to individual retailers, however the companies listed below do sell directly to retailers.

Again, the National Bridal Markets (**http://nationalbridalmarket.com**) is the best place to meet industry representatives. Just as it is with wholesalers, the National Bridal Market offers the best place to meet industry manufacturers' and designers' representatives, as hundreds have display booths at these events. Another way to find out which designers are best to deal with is to visit the manufacturers' forum on the Wedding Industry website at **www.weddingindustry.com**.

Here is a selection of inventory suppliers recommended by bridal salon experts we consulted.

- *Aalexis Wedding Accessories*
  www.aalexis.com

- *Alfred Sung Bridals*
  www.alfredsungbridals.com

- *Bliss Bridal Shoes*
  www.blissbridalshoes.com

- *Dessy Group*
  (Gowns and accessories)
  www.dessy.com/retailers/

- *Dyeables*
  (Shoes and handbags)
  www.Dyeables.com

- *Forever Yours Bridals*
  www.foreverbridals.com

- *House of Wu*
  www.houseofwu.com

- *Maggie Sottero*
  www.maggiesottero.com

- *Mon Cheri Bridals*
  www.mcbridals.com

- *Mori Lee*
  (Click on "About", then on "Retailer Policy".)
  www.morilee.com

- *Private Label by G*
  www.privatelabelbyg.com

- *Winnie Couture*
  (Click on the "Business Partner" link.)
  www.winniecouture.com

4.5.4   Prices and Terms

Manufacturers and wholesalers typically have suggested retail prices and offer discounts based on quantities purchased. In the wedding industry, it's usual for manufacturers to insist on a minimum order of at least six gowns per season (spring and fall). You'll have to buy these gowns outright to use them as samples in your store, but unworn merchandise can typically be returned within 90 days, unless it's sold to you as part of a discounted sale by the manufacturer—in which case it can't be returned.

When your customer orders a gown, you'll need to pay the supplier for the order right away. That's why you need to ask the customer for half of the price of her gown, up front.

Here are some questions to consider when considering your suppliers' prices and terms:

- Are the prices and terms the company is offering acceptable? Ask the vendor to tell you all the charges that will be involved with a purchase. In addition to the price of the product, there may be taxes, delivery charges, duties for items coming from another country, rush charges, etc. If you are dealing with a wholesaler, you should ask about "up charges" (a fee on top of the manufacturer's price).

- What discount will you receive off the retail price? Typical discounts when buying wholesale (i.e. from the manufacturer) are 20-50%. You may need a copy of your retail license to get the wholesale rate or to avoid paying sales tax.

- When is payment required? If you do not have a business history, most vendors will want to be paid for items before they ship them. Many times you will not be able to purchase wholesale using your credit card, so you will need to have funds readily available to cover your purchases with a check.

- What about over-runs or under-runs? While manufacturers normally do their best to ensure they deliver exactly what you have ordered, many include in their contract that they can ship 10-15% over or under the amount ordered.

TIP: Make sure you read any sales contracts carefully and have them reviewed by your lawyer to ensure you are protected.

4.5.5   Consignment

If you are running a second-hand bridal store or are willing to consider offering some consigned merchandise, one of the best ways to add merchandise to your inventory is from consignors. Taking in items on consignment is a good way to get new merchandise without having to spend any of your own money. As Susan Alexander Shapiro, founder of BravoBride, a leading online retailer of second-hand gowns, says, "Our main sources of inventory are newlyweds and brides who bought more than one wedding gown, too many items for their wedding, or have leftover items."

Because many young brides are Internet-savvy, they may buy their dresses online to begin with, whether it's from gown exchange-type sites like BravoBride or from independent sellers on sites like eBay—or they buy them new, direct from manufacturers or online stores. This is an excellent "secret" source of consignment items for your store, because often these garments do not fit exactly or cannot be returned. Consider advertising your consignment needs in places like Google, where brides may be searching for dresses to buy online.

Remember that consigned merchandise doesn't have to be second-hand merchandise. You might very well find that there is an up-and-coming designer in your area who is looking for a place to showcase his or her wedding or formal gown designs. If there is a college offering fashion design courses in your area, consider contacting them to make arrangements to have some of their students showcase their work in your store. This could lead to a very lucrative partnership over time.

A few reasons to consider a consignment item:

- The item is great and would be too expensive for you to buy outright.
- You know you can make some money on the item.
- The item cannot be easily stolen, damaged, or broken.

Items you consign should be desirable and priced to sell. You do not want to be a storage unit for customers. Make sure when you consign that you both agree on the price and how you will make money on the item. In order to make the most of this arrangement, you will need to have a consignment policy.

Ask the consignor what they want to get out of the item. If it is a reasonable price leaving you room to mark up the item and make money then you might consider doing the consignment. Consignments to refuse are those where either you know the items aren't saleable or owners want an unrealistic amount of money for them.

If you do accept a consignment, you and the item's owner will decide together what to price the item at. From that sale price, you will take an agreed percentage of the sale, usually 10, 20, or 50 percent. As a rule, the more expensive the item, the smaller percentage you will take on the sale.

Put all consignment agreements in writing. Include length and dates of consignment, what the consignor wants to net from the item and a disclaimer that you are not responsible for fire, theft or any damage.

However you decide to set up your consignment arrangements with customers, make sure you have something in writing to be signed by the consignor. You should consider having an attorney draw up a consignment agreement for your store. Like any contract, you and the consignor can cross things out and add other information and details that you both agree on. Make sure you both sign the contract and each of you has a signed copy.

There are several things you will want to be sure to address in your consignment policy. These rules should be posted clearly as well as distributed to customers and consignors.

Be sure to include:

- When you will accept items for consignment. Be specific here. There may be seasonal items you don't want to deal with when they are out of season, for example.

- Do they need an appointment to bring their consignments in?

- What types of items do you accept? Again, be specific. If you only accept certain kinds of items and specifically exclude others, then state that on your policy.

- What condition should the items be in?

- Do you limit the number of items from a single consignor? State that in your policy.

- How much commission will they earn? When will they get paid or receive credits?

- Unsold items—can they pick them up? By appointment or anytime?

- Discount schedule—Do you discount items that have been in your store after a certain period of time? How do you determine this?

- Responsibilities—What happens if a consigned item is stolen?

Sample Consignment Policy

Something Old, Something New Bridal Salon is happy to accept your gown for consignment.

We will accept your gown during regular business hours, Monday through Saturday, 10:00 a.m. to 7:00 p.m.

We accept wedding gowns, formal gowns, tuxedos, and accessories like handbags and shoes. These items must be brought in good condition, professionally cleaned and with no tears, stains or flaws. We reserve the right to refuse any gown for consignment, based on our opinion of what we will be able to sell.

You will receive 40% of the selling price if the item sells within 90 days.

Time Period:	Discount Rate:
91-120 days	25 percent discount to buyer
121-150 days	50 percent discount to buyer
151-180 days	75 percent discount to buyer

Your unsold items may be picked up anytime after the initial 90-day period. You will be asked to pull your own items, but they should be clearly marked and our sales associates will direct you to the correct area of the store.

We look forward to working with you and welcome you to Something Old, Something New Bridal.

Our store is not liable for loss of consigned items due to fire, theft, natural disasters or any other unforeseen circumstance.

5. Running Your Business

5.1 Store Operations

Your daily operations will run more smoothly if you develop a clear set of policies and procedures to follow, both for you and for your staff. Remember, you won't necessarily know how everything should be right away, and that your Procedures Manual will be a work in progress for the first while. Also remember, it's not written in stone. If someone comes up with a better way to do something, you can always change the manual.

5.1.1 Developing a Procedures Manual

As you move through the process of opening your store, you will begin to notice that you are starting to develop routines around how you do various things. These routines will fall eventually under the more official business term —operations. One of the great things about owning your own store is that you are in charge of deciding the routines of your operations, and you can plan how things run in your store to satisfy your needs and desires.

Every time you do something new, keep a record of how you did it. As you go along, take accurate notes about what works, what doesn't work, and what will need to be done a different way. Over time you will begin to see an organized system emerge — this is the beginning of the development of your operational procedures.

Having written records and instructions of important store procedures and tasks makes it possible for your employees to complete tasks more efficiently by themselves. Also, store procedures aren't necessarily things that you can (or even want to) store in your head. It is hard to remember all the passwords and codes for things, the procedures for receiving merchandise, or the steps in taking a check from a customer. The best thing to do is to make a guide for employees (and for you) to keep this information organized and accessible.

Putting together an operations manual for your store will help you get all of your procedures and instructions for every little task organized and in one spot for you and your employees to refer to. Follow the simple directions below to make your own Store Operations Manual.

What You Need

Here are the things you'll need to create your manual:

- Checklists for each area of the store (see below for some sample checklists)

- Three-ring binder or folder with clear plastic insert space on cover and spine

- Three-hole punch

- Binder dividers with section labels

- Checklist forms

- Task forms

- Special reminder forms

- Emergency forms

What to Do

Once you have gathered your materials, follow these steps:

- Carefully consider each area of your operations. Make divider tags for the binder with the following labels: Opening Tasks, Closing Tasks, Daily Tasks, Weekly Tasks, Monthly Tasks, Quarterly Tasks, Annual Tasks. Place these labeled dividers in the binder.

- Make a checklist for each area. Use the checklist examples on the following pages to get started. List the tasks that you can think of for each area. Remember to write down important reminder information like where things are located, which lights to turn on, etc. Think about how you would instruct someone unfamiliar with the task to do it. Sequentially ordered steps work the best.

- Fill out a separate sequential form or reminder sheet for each specific area of operations in your store.

- Make a list of emergency number and other emergency information for the first page of the binder. You might want to place a copy of every employee's emergency information card inside the binder directly behind the emergency number and procedure page.

- Label the binder clearly and make a copy of all the contents to store in a safe place away from your store.

TIP: Remember that this operations manual will be fluid and will change over time. As you change your procedures, remember to change the corresponding task page.

5.1.2   Areas of Operations Checklists

Here are some examples of various areas of the store and some things in each area that you might want to include in your operations manual:

Opening/Closing

- ❑ Door locks
- ❑ Lights — both indoor and outdoor
- ❑ Security systems and codes
- ❑ What to do if the alarm goes off accidentally
- ❑ Turning on/off the air-conditioning and heating units
- ❑ Turning on/off computers/fax/postal machine/copier
- ❑ Mail sorting and opening
- ❑ Brewing coffee
- ❑ Email
- ❑ Answering machine
- ❑ Cleaning break room and staff kitchen area

Cash Wrap

- ❑ Operating the cash register
- ❑ Preparing money drawer for opening
- ❑ Processing credit and debit cards
- ❑ Processing checks
- ❑ Accepting and selling gift certificates
- ❑ Completing a transaction
- ❑ Keeping track of what is sold/inventory
- ❑ Phone procedures
- ❑ Directions to store
- ❑ Using computers/fax/postal machine/copier
- ❑ Mailing list

❏ Promotions and sales

❏ Cash deposits and bank deposits

❏ Wrapping gifts

Merchandise and Sales

❏ Procedures for receiving inventory

❏ Procedures for contacting clients when their orders have arrived

❏ Procedures for first fitting/alterations

❏ Where to find consignment forms

❏ Creating consignment cards

❏ Pricing merchandise

❏ Putting tags on items

❏ Shelving merchandise

❏ Making displays

❏ Cleaning and organizing displays

❏ Answering customer questions

❏ When to discount prices on merchandise

❏ Handling refunds

❏ Pulling unsold items to return to the consignor

❏ Donating unsold items to charity

Safety/Health/Emergency Procedures

❏ Emergency contact numbers—fire, police, hospitals, etc

❏ Staff and owner emergency contact numbers

❏ Procedures for emergency in-store illness—for both staff members and customers

❑ Evacuation procedures

❑ Emergency or natural disaster plan

❑ What to do in case of shoplifting

❑ What to do in case of robbery

5.2 Inventory Management

5.2.1 Inventory Software

Ask ten different store owners what inventory system they use to track sales and you will likely get ten different answers. There are a few owners still keeping track of items by hand; however, eventually most retail stores have to use some sort of software as sales volumes increase.

There are a wide variety of options available to store owners. Which software works best is often a personal choice and depends on the type of store, the size of store, and how many customers you have.

This is a big investment, so take your time. Fortunately, many of these software programs offer a free demo trial period, so you can try out several different versions before deciding which one you would like to purchase. Try the various demos. Find out which program works best for you before using up valuable hours punching in information on products, only to realize the software you purchased is not working to meet your needs.

> "When looking for software, try before you buy! Take advantage of the various free demos and talk to the people supporting it. The typical user wants, and needs, the availability of program updates and ongoing assistance when needed."
>
> — Bill Hawkins, Computer Consultants Exchange

After reviewing the various types of software, there are several that stand out as easy to use and filled with great features. Here are just a few of the choices available to you in a range of prices, including an example of consignment software:

- *BBL Systems*
  Software designed especially for the bridal wear and tuxedo rental industry, by a company that's been in business more than 20 years. You can buy, rent or lease this software package, which means less initial outlay. Use it to track inventory, manage staff time, book appointments, make sales and more. Software package starts at $1,999, but can be customized and expanded to accommodate any number of computers or stores. Also offers an online version, for an access fee of $100/month. An industry favourite.
  www.bblsystems.com/start.htm

- *Bridal Web Solutions*
  Online software that lets you track sales, manage inventory and customer databases, order supplies, keep track of staff time and more. You can try it out with a free demo.
  www.bridalwebsolutions.ca

- *Dressprice*
  For a $149 initial set-up fee and a membership fee of $14.99 a month (U.S.D), you can use this online service to track inventory, manage layaway and special orders, keep customer mailing lists and customize the system to meet your needs. You can see a free demo at the website and sign up for a free trial as well.
  www.dressprice.com

- *Consignment Shop Software*
  Starts at about $400 and offers 60-90 days of free support. Offers two versions. One is more for clothing stores, the other for stores with a variety of items, including big-ticket items such as furniture.
  www.consignmentshopsoftware.com

"Acquiring an inventory management point-of-sale system is important, because it helps you set yourself apart from your competition. You'll look much more professional in the eyes of your customers."

> — Sidney Green, Vice-president, software sales,
> BBL Systems

5.2.2   Inventory Tags and Labels

To keep track of inventory some stores use simple tags they label by hand, while others use bar code tags that work with whatever type of software they are using. You should use whatever system makes the most sense for your store.

If your store is organized neatly and your prices are marked clearly, not only will shopping be easier and more comfortable for customers, you will find that keeping track of your inventory is easier. Using inventory systems to keep organized will help you avoid the frustration of not being able to find inventory or a special order.

Most retail stores use either simple labels with neat, handwritten prices or printed price stickers from a pricing gun or computer printer. You might consider self-adhesive labels, but be careful with them. Some labels leave glue residue on items and will sometimes cause a permanent mark when removed. Many retailers use string tags that they can tie onto merchandise. Use these for larger, more visible items because some people might be tempted to remove a higher price tag and replace it with a lower price one.

Some retailers use bar code tags that work with whatever type of software and scanner they use. Although initially more expensive than stickers or string tags, if you get very busy the time you save keeping track of your inventory might easily pay for it. Your choice of which system to use will largely depend on the type of inventory you carry and your inventory turnover.

To find out more about labeling and bar code systems you can visit Motorola Retail Solutions at **www.symbol.com/retail** or POSWorld. com, both of which offer labels, inventory management and bar code systems. Most office supply stores like Staples, Office Depot, and Office Max, sell string tags, price stickers, and pricing guns.

5.3   Pricing Merchandise

This section explains the different ways retailers determine the sale price of their goods. The bridal industry operates with a basic 100 percent markup (retail price is twice what it cost wholesale), but there are variations to take into account. Those variations are explained here.

5.3.1 Guidelines

One main consideration for pricing items is what the local market will bear. If certain items are in high demand then you'll probably be able to charge higher prices for those. This is the "law" of supply and demand and you should pay close attention to any trends you see developing in your customers' buying patterns to take advantage of this.

Here are some basic tips for pricing your items:

- Consider what the market will bear. A store in an upscale area may allow you to price your items a bit higher.

- Consider your competition. Are there any other stores like yours in the area? What are they charging for similar items? If you are selling products such as shoes, make sure you can price items comparatively against Wal-Mart or similar superstores.

- It is not always best to price items lower than the competition charges. Most people believe you get what you pay for. The key is to price the item fairly but allow yourself a reasonable profit.

- Items in a particular section of the retail industry have a certain perceived value. What are customers willing to pay for the item? What is it worth to them?

Another trick most stores use is to price things just under the dollar mark. For example, instead of putting a price of $10 on an item, you would mark it $9.99. Even though there is only a penny's difference between the two prices, customers will perceive one as ten dollars and the other as nine dollars, resulting in better sales.

Clearing Items Out

You have to do something with items that do not sell. You will find that some items, even though they seemed like a good choice for your store when you bought them, just won't sell. How long will you wait until the cost of carrying an item on your shelf exceeds what you originally paid for it? Sometimes it's better to cut your losses and get at least something for such merchandise.

Clearance racks or tables are a good place to start. Many retailers also offer slow selling merchandise for sale during sidewalk sales or other similar promotions. Make sure that you're offering good bargains, too, when you do this or customers will see that you're just trying to get rid of tired merchandise. Put new price stickers or tags on the merchandise and dust it if needed.

Your discount schedule is a matter of individual preference. Some owners leave their items at full price until 90 days or longer have passed or until the items are no longer in season. They then discount the items (e.g. by 20%) or offer them as" buy two get one free" or even "buy one get one free." Obviously, only a highly undecided bride would want to buy two wedding gowns in order to get a third free, however, this strategy could work with wedding party wear, shoes for the wedding party, or jewelry items.

5.3.2   Retail Pricing Formulas

There are different methods that retailers use to arrive at their prices. Many manufacturers have a suggested retail price (MSRP) for retailers to follow. These are found along with their wholesale price to the retailer in their product catalogs. You can choose to follow a MSRP or not. The important questions to ask are whether the MSRP allows you sufficient profit and is it priced too high for your market. If the answer is no to the first and yes to the second, you might want to look for a different supplier.

A more efficient and profitable way to price is using a retail pricing formula. Generally, there are two concepts retailers should be aware of: percentage margin and price markup. Using these formulas will tell you what your percentage of profit is based on the percentage markup above your wholesale (i.e. purchase) price for that item. If the profit percentage is too low, then you'll want to use a different price markup percentage for that item.

As an example of how pricing affects your business, we'll use the break-even point for a fictional business. You may remember the formula for calculating the break-even point from section 3.4.2 as:

$$\text{Break-even point} = \text{Total fixed costs}/$$
$$(1 - \text{total variable costs}/\text{revenues}).$$

In the example in section 3.4.2, the break-even point for the business was $69,000 in annual revenues. Also, for every dollar of sales, the company had 56 cents in variable expenses. Therefore, to break even, fixed costs can represent no more than 44 cents on every dollar. So if you had an item priced at $1.00, 56% of the selling price would be variable expenses and the rest would be fixed costs, leaving no room for profit. Obviously, nobody wants to run their store like that.

Based on these figures, the store owner might want to increase the profit margin. So for example, instead of selling a product for $1.00 as before, the owner might increase the retail price to $1.25. This would lower the percentage for each of fixed and variable costs as a percentage of revenue, resulting in an increased profit margin.

5.3.3 Profit Margin vs. Percentage Markup

Every retailer needs to understand the difference between profit margin and percentage markup. The profit margin is the amount of your retail price that represents profit for you over and above the cost of the merchandise. In a more sophisticated model, you would also include your total operating expenses as well. You would add in your fixed and variable costs and factor them into your pricing model, along with cost of goods.

The percentage markup is the percentage amount you increased the retail price over your cost for a given item. After you have been in business for a while, you will know what price markup generally works best for you. Pricing by percentage markup is less usual than pricing by profit margin.

Let's look at a specific example. Consider an item with a retail price of $1.00, that the owner paid 40 cents for. The profit margin formula is:

$$
\begin{aligned}
\text{Margin} &= (1 - (\text{cost} \div \text{selling})) \times 100 \\
&= (1 - (40 \div 100)) \times 100 \\
&= (1 - .40) \times 100 \\
&= .60 \times 100 \\
&= 60
\end{aligned}
$$

So in this example the profit margin is 60%.

If, however, you decided that you would set your prices by marking up everything by 60%, then the percentage markup formula is:

$$\text{Price} = \text{cost} + (\text{cost} \times 60 \div 100)$$
$$= 40 + (40 \times 0.60)$$
$$= 40 + 24$$
$$= 64$$

Using a fixed markup of 60%, the retail price on an item costing $0.40 would be $0.64.

Look carefully at these two formulas. Notice that markup pricing and profit margin pricing create two very different selling prices. In the first example, pricing based on a 60% profit margin required a selling price of $1.00. In the second example, using a percentage markup of 60% on cost resulted in a price of only 64 cents, a profit margin of only about 38%.

A quick way to calculate a profit margin price is to divide the cost price by the difference between 100 and the profit margin. For example, if you wanted to have a 5% profit margin you would divide your cost price by (100-5) or 95 percent. So if you paid 40 cents for a product and you wanted a 5% profit margin, to arrive at your selling price you would use the formula: 40/(100-5) = 40/.95 = 42 cents. Here are some additional examples so you can see the trend:

10%: 40 ÷ (100 - 10) = 44 cents
15%: 40 ÷ (100 - 15) = 47 cents
25%: 40 ÷ (100 - 25) = 53 cents
50%: 40 ÷ (100 - 50) = 80 cents

Once you know your cost of doing business, you can easily arrive at a minimum profit percentage margin price that will meet your needs. You'll also be able to look at a MSRP and determine if it meets your profit margin requirements.

Keep some of the other pricing concepts in mind as well. Your market may be able to support a higher profit margin in your pricing. Alternatively, you might be able to split margins by pricing higher ticket, lower volume items at a lower profit percentage, and use a higher profit margin on merchandise that sells for a lower price but at a higher volume.

Another way to increase your profit margin is to reduce your variable expenses. If you find that your profit margin is too low, you can reduce costs like labor, store supplies, or even look for lower cost wholesale merchandise.

To read more about retail pricing concepts, try the following online resources:

- *Markup or Margin: Selling and Pricing*
  www.buildingtrade.org.uk/articles/markup_or_margin.html

- *Margin Markup/Profit Percentage Table*
  www.csgnetwork.com/marginmarkuptable.html

- *Pricing Your Products and Services Profitably*
  (Click on "Financial Management Series" and look for #7.)
  www.sba.gov/tools/resourcelibrary/publications/index.html

5.3.4 Standard Markups

When you purchase your inventory from wholesalers, designers, and manufacturers, you pay less than your customers will pay you for the same merchandise. This difference is your gross profit margin. Typically, your profit margin is 50%, which means that for every dollar you bring in on a retail sale you will earn fifty cents above the wholesale price you paid for that product. Some manufacturers control the pricing of their products by giving a suggested retail price (MSRP). This means they will sell the gown to you wholesale at a discounted price that's about half the MSRP. So, a gown that you charge your customer $300 for will cost you about $150, or a 50% discount.

Typically, pricing your products is a matter of doubling the price you paid wholesale. For accessories and shoes, you may want to increase the retail price to one and a half times your wholesale price. Some bridal salons add an additional amount (typically $100 to $300) to the cost of each dress to cover shipping costs, especially if the gowns are made overseas. When this cost is built into the cost of the gown, stores advertise "free shipping" because shipping fees are not added onto the top of the purchase price. This creates the perception of additional service value.

Following is a sample price list for products typically sold in bridal salons.

Sample Price List

Bridal wear and accessories

Item:	Cost:
Off-the-rack gown	$399.00
Custom-designed gown	$1,250.00-$1,500.00
Bridal veil	$150.00
Dyeable satin shoes	$95.00
Corset	$120.00
Handbag, beaded	$60.00
Tiara (rhinestone)	$90.00-$145.00 (depending on complexity)
Alterations	$30.00-$50.00/hour
Shoe dyeing service	$20.00-$40.00/pair

Alterations are an important part of your pricing structure. If you do alterations in-house, you will charge by the hour for your seamstress' services. This cost is typically $30 to $50 an hour, depending on your seamstress's skills and the complexity of the work. Altering a complicated bodice will cost more, for example, than taking up a simple hem.

For custom work, in which you or your staff produce the entire dress from start to finish, the pricing formula is more complicated. One bridal salon owner we talked with explains her pricing formula for her custom work as follows:

"We take the cost of materials and an hourly wage for our work and double it for a total price. Say that you spend $100 on the fabric, $200 on trim and $200 on other items such as threads, beading, etc. Then you spend 20 hours to cut, piece and sew the item. Say you charge $30 [per hour] for your services or someone else's services if they have to do detailed beading etc. Then multiply by 2 for your cut, which would go toward your profit, advertising, time and business costs. [The manufactured cost] comes to $1,100 and then doubled is $2,200."

— Karen Caprio, Bellina Bridal, New York City

Custom Design Gown Pricing Worksheet

Cost of fabric: _____

Cost of trims: _____

Cost of notions: _____

Cost of labor*:

_____ hours at $____/hour   = _____

Subtotal: _____

Multiply by 2:   x2

Total Cost of Gown $_____

* Cost of labor could include the time it takes you to measure the bride and design the gown specifically for her, as well as the time it takes to assemble and fit the finished gown.

5.4 Getting Paid

As soon as you establish your business you will need to open a business checking account at a bank, trust company, or credit union. You can shop around to find a financial institution that is supportive of small business, or use the same one that you use for your personal banking.

In addition to your checking account, a financial institution may provide you with a corporate credit card used to make purchases for your business, a line of credit to purchase items for your store, and a merchant credit card account enabling you to accept credit card payments from customers.

You have a variety of options for getting paid by your customers.

5.4.1 Accepting Debit Cards

With a debit purchase, the funds come directly out of the customer's account at the bank and are deposited directly into your business bank account. There is no credit involved for customer or merchant. In order to set up debit payment, you will need to ask your bank for an application and you will need a debit machine. The equipment costs about $200 to $500, but some companies offer leases.

There may be a short delay or small charge to you, initially or ongoing, depending on the bank. And you will have to get the equipment to process the payments and print receipts. (Federal law mandates receipts be provided to customers for debit card purchases.) To find out more about debit card services in the U.S., visit the Electronic Transactions Association directory of member companies at **www.electran.org** (click on "Information Resources" then "Links to Industry Web Sites"), or in Canada, visit the Interac Association at **www.interac.org**.

5.4.2 Accepting Credit Cards

American Express and Discover cards set up merchant accounts nationally and internationally. MasterCard and Visa are local. To become a merchant accepting MasterCard and Visa, you will have to get accepted by a local acquirer (a financial institution like a bank licensed by the credit card company). Because yours is a new business, you may have to shop around to find one that gives you good rates (you may be charged between 1.5 and 3 percent per transaction for the service, and often an initial setup fee and perhaps ongoing fees for phone calls, postage, statements, and so on).

You might also have to provide evidence of a good personal financial record to set up an advantageous rate, at least until you've become established in your business and have a good track record for them to look at. Remember, the bank is granting you credit in this instance, "banking" on the fact that your customers will not want refunds or that you won't try to keep the money if they do.

These days, although the acquiring bank will be a local bank somewhere, it need not be in your hometown. Numerous services are available online to help you set up a merchant account. MasterCard and Visa accounts, as well as American Express and Discover, can all be set up through your local bank or by going to the websites of each of these companies.

- *MasterCard Merchant*
  www.mastercard.com/us/merchant
  www.mastercard.com/ca/merchant/en/index.html

- *Visa*
  http://usa.visa.com/merchants/merchant_resources/
  www.visa.ca/en/merchant/

- *American Express*
  https://home.americanexpress.com/
  homepage/merchant_ne.shtml?

- *Discover*
  www.discovernetwork.com/discovernetwork/
  howitworks/howitworks.html

5.4.3   Accepting Payment Online

If you have a website you can accept payments online through services such as PayPal (**www.paypal.com**). Typically, these services charge a greater "discount rate," which is what the 1.5 to 3 percent the banks and credit card companies hold from your payments is called. And the purchase must be made online. Still, there may be instances when you are doing business online with some of your clients, and it may be useful then. Also, it provides a safe route for conveying financial information over the Internet.

5.4.4   Accepting Checks

When you accept checks, especially to cover big-ticket items or major corporate purchases, you may want to have a back-up system for getting paid if the customer has insufficient funds in their checking account. It's important to get a credit card number, driver's license number, and full phone number and address (you might even want to check it online quickly to insure they are legitimate). If you have any doubts as to their honesty, it might be a good idea not to accept the check and let the sale go.

You can accept checks from customers with greater assurance by using a check payment service such as TeleCheck. TeleCheck compares checks you receive with a database of over 51 million bad check records, allowing you to decide whether to accept a check from a particular client. The company also provides electronic payment services, from telephone debit card processing to electronic checks. You can find out more about TeleCheck at **www.telecheck.com**.

5.4.5   Accepting Deposits and Down Payments

Wedding gowns are expensive, often custom-made garments that require extra attention to detail and a large initial outlay, even for the retailer who orders them. To accommodate this fact, bridal salons typically require their clients to pay a "deposit" or "down payment" when the gown is first ordered.

This amount is usually 50 percent of the cost of the gown (the amount needed to pay the wholesaler for the order), with the balance required when the gown arrives at the salon and before the first fitting. If a gown is particularly expensive, a salon might charge up to 65 percent of the total for the down payment. Still others offer a modest (five percent) discount for cash payment, or payment in full, if the client pays up front for the whole amount. This helps ensure that the store does not end up with merchandise from a supplier that hasn't been paid for in full. Some salons charge a per-month "storage fee" if the balance remains unpaid for more than a month after the gown arrives at the salon.

> TIP: Many bridal salon owners suggest calling this payment a down payment or partial payment, because in some places a "deposit" implies that the money will be returned. You could also call it a "nonrefundable deposit."

To help clients who find it hard to make the full payment all at once, some salons offer a monthly payment plan. To determine this amount, divide the balance of the cost (after the first initial 50 percent payment) by the number of months between order and delivery, and let the client pay that amount each month. For example, if a gown costs $1,000, and the initial down payment was $500, the remaining $500 could be divided between the five months between January, when the order was placed, and May, when the gown will arrive at the store. This means that the client would pay $125/month until her gown is ready, at which time it will be paid for in full.

Following is a sample sales contract that you can use when clients order a dress. It's a good idea to post this sales agreement (or at least the details of your terms of purchase) at your cash desk and in your dressing rooms, to let clients know exactly what the rules are.

Sample Sales Contract

Something Old, Something New Bridal Salon
1234 Pleasant Street
Evervile, CA 99999
555-555-1234

Client name: _____

Order number: _____

Order description: _____

Price:_____

Down payment: $_____   Paid on: _____(date)

Balance remaining: $_____   Due on: _____(date)

**All deposits, payments and special orders are
FINAL and NON-REFUNDABLE.
Invoice due on receipt.**

NO refunds, exchanges or store credit on custom orders.

I agree to pay 50 percent of my full order value on ordering, and the balance within 10 days of receiving notification that my order has arrived.

Customer signature: _____

Date:_____

5.5 Financial Management

5.5.1 Bookkeeping

We did not speak to a single store owner who enjoyed keeping books, but all of them stressed the importance of doing so. Maintaining accurate, up-to-date records can help you run your business more cost-effectively and efficiently. By keeping track of how much everything costs, you'll quickly know what marketing efforts don't pay off, and what types of pieces are not worth bringing in.

Keeping your books includes tracking two things:

- How much money you have coming in

- How much money you have going out

Bookkeeping Systems

Some people prefer to keep track of everything manually. Many business owners simply buy a few journals, write their accounts across the top and enter each month's expenses by hand. This method works well if you are organized, and love the feel of pen on paper. But if you have employees, several sources of income, and a steady flow of traffic through your store, you'll soon forget a few months, and it will become a monster lying in wait for you in your desk's bottom drawer.

Luckily for small business owners, there are several fairly inexpensive software systems that can easily guide you through the bookkeeping process. Intuit offers different types of financial software for different types of businesses. Intuit's Quickbooks, one of the most popular bookkeeping systems, can run about $800 with point of sale functions, but will quickly pay for itself in the savings of not hiring a full-time bookkeeper. Intuit also offers a basic program, Quicken Home & Business, which is a good option for new businesses and costs about $80.

Another maker of business management software is Acclivity (formerly MYBO). Their "Premier Accounting" suite allows you to track revenues and expenses, record bank deposits, generate reports, track customers and more. There are several other financial programs, including Accpac and Simply Accounting which you can find at your local office supplies store.

- Acclivity Premier Accounting
  www.myob-us.com/businessbasics/

- Quicken
  http://quicken.intuit.com

- Quickbooks
  http://quickbooks.intuit.com

- Simply Accounting
  www.simplyaccounting.com

Even though software can make most of the work easier for you, you might consider taking a beginning accounting or a bookkeeping class at a local community college. Accounting basics are vital information that all store owners need, but sometimes neglect to learn. Even if you hire someone to do your books, you'll need to know the basics so that you can understand what is going on in your accounts.

You might consider hiring a part-time bookkeeper on a contract basis if you find yourself so busy running your store that you don't have time to do your books yourself. Depending on how busy you are, it may take the bookkeeper a few hours per week to get your books up to date and balance them with your bank statements. You can find a bookkeeper through word of mouth or the Yellow Pages.

Even if you plan on having a fulltime bookkeeper or accountant, you should know enough about your store's books to be able to do them yourself if you need to, and certainly to be able to check the accuracy and honesty of those whom you employ. You should know how to:

- Make a daily sales report of the money you take in each day

- Make accounts payable and accounts receivable reports

- Make and read an income statement (also called a profit and loss statement)

- Make and read a cash flow statement

- Understand a balance sheet

The following sections will help you to understand more about these business basics.

5.5.2   Financial Statements and Reports

The Daily Sales Report

Every day you take in money. You get cash, you take credit cards, and possibly debit cards for payment, and you may even accept checks. A daily sales report logs all of this information. It will also help you ready the monies you take in for your bank deposit. Most accounting software will allow you to enter this information. Some booksellers do this by hand—they create or buy a form to use and put the daily proceeds in an envelope. You will want to check your cash register receipts against what you actually have in your cash drawer to make sure it all matches at the end of each day.

Most accounting software will provide this type of report or you can do the report by hand. On the next page is an example of a daily sales tracking report.

> TIP: Balance your cash register float every day to your sales tracking report. (The "float" is the cash you start your day with in order to make change.)

Your Sales Pace

A good way to determine if your sales for the month are on track on any given day is to follow your sales pace. At any time during the month, this will tell you what you can expect to earn for the remainder of the month. Perhaps a big snow storm has caused a sales slump for several days during the week. How much will you need to earn for the rest of the month to meet your revenue target?

The basic formula for calculating sales pace is:

Sales Pace = (Total Sales/Number of Business Days so far for the month) x the number of business days in the month

From the Daily Sales Report above, the store did $18,000 up to the 13th business day of the month. The sales pace is calculated using the preceding 12 days of sales as: $18,000/12 x 31 = $1,500 x 31 = $46,500.

Sample Daily Sales Report

Date: October 13, 20___

	Today	Month to Date
Cash	$1,319.10	$18,000.00
Checks	515.85	7,200.00
Master Card	180.04	2,400.00
Visa	$70.26	1,200.00
Other	0	400.00
Store Credit	0	0.00
Subtotal	**$2,085.25**	**$29,200.00**
Starting Float (Subtract)	(-250.00)	(-250.00)
Deposit Total	**$1,835.25**	**$28,950.00**
Returns	0	178.75
Voids	0	43.92
Pay Outs	0	250.00
Other	0	0
Total Cash Paid Out	**0**	**472.67**
Deposit Total Less Total Cash Paid Out	**$1,835.25**	**$28,477.33**
Sales Tax Collected	91.76	1,447.50
Cash Register Reading	$1,834.25	$28,477.65
Difference (+ or -)	$1.00	$0.32

So, for the entire month at the current sales pace, the store can expect around $47,000 in sales. If the store owner had projected $45,000 in sales for this month, then the sales pace is well on track. If the projection was $50,000, then sales are a bit behind.

Another point to consider is that sales on the 13th day of the month were above the average daily sales ($1,835 as compared to $1,500). The store owner can figure out now what the sales pace for the rest of the month will need to be to maintain the target pace.

Let's say the store owner had projected $50,000 in sales for the month. To calculate the sales pace that is needed for the remainder of the month, use the formula:

$$\text{Sales pace} = (\$50{,}000 - (\$1{,}500 \times 12))/18 = \$1{,}778$$

The store will need to produce $1,778 in sales each day for the remaining 18 days of the month in order to reach the $50,000 sales target for the month. Based on the preceding 12 days of sales, the store is a bit behind in its daily and month-to-date target sales.

Income Statement (Profit and Loss Statement)

Your income statement (also called a profit and loss or P&L statement) will tell you how much money you have in expenses and how much money you have in revenue for a given period. A number of things are necessary for an income statement.

You'll need to know:

- Your revenues for the period (gross sales minus returns and discounts)

- The cost of goods sold (what it cost you during the period to purchase merchandise for your store for the period)

- Your gross profit (revenues minus cost of goods sold)

- Your operating expenses (everything you must pay for to operate your store, including non-cash items like depreciation)

- Your net profit before and after taxes (revenues minus your operating expenses, and then subtract your tax liability)

The end result will tell you how much money your store is making — what is commonly referred to as "the bottom line."

You will want to decide which method of accounting you want to use, accrual method or cash method. In the accrual method, income is reported in the month it is earned and expenses reported in the month they are incurred (even if they have not yet been paid).

The cash method tracks actual money received and actual money spent. You do not consider any outstanding bills or invoices. The Business Owner's Toolkit website has an article entitled "Cash vs. Accrual Accounting" at **www.toolkit.cch.com/text/P06_1340.asp** that you can read as an introduction to this topic.

On the next page is an example of a typical income statement.

Cash Flow Statement

The cash flow statement allows you to quickly see whether more cash is coming in than going out, or vice versa, at the end of each month. It also allows you to make projections for certain periods of the year (such as the summer months when you might have increased sales due to larger numbers of tourists in your area at that time), or project cash flow year-over-year, and budget accordingly. You can also use it to track monthly cash flow and make projections for the coming month. This is handy if you're planning to make a large equipment or inventory purchase and need to know if you can afford it.

Cash flow is an important element of your financial picture. Monitoring cash flow lets you see how well your business is doing from day to day. Are you paying expenses with the money you take in from your operating revenues, or are you paying for expenses with other business funds such as banked working capital? If you are doing so with the former, your business is self-sustaining.

To keep track of expenses, you will need to keep copies of all receipts. This can be a challenge for new business owners who might have a habit of tossing out receipts for small items or not asking for receipts in the first place. However, you are likely to have numerous small expenses related to your business, and these can add up over time. These expenses should be accounted for so you can minimize your taxes. And, of course, knowing exactly where your money is going will help you plan better and cut back on any unnecessary expenses. So make it a habit to ask for a receipt for every expense related to your business.

You can see a sample six-month cash flow worksheet for the first six months of operation following the sample income statement on the next page.

Sample Income Statement

Income Statement [Company Name]
for month ending July 31, 20__

REVENUE ($)	
Cash sales	5,250
Credit card sales	1,600
Online sales	150
Total Sales	**$7,000**

COST OF GOODS SOLD	
Inventory and material purchases	1,800
Shipping	50
Supplies	150
Total cost of goods sold	**$2,000**

GROSS PROFIT	$5,000

EXPENSES	
Lease	1,850
Insurance	75
Licenses & taxes	250
Office supplies & postage	100
Interest	95
Utilities	225
Wages	550
Telephone and Internet	115
Depreciation	55
Vehicle expenses	220
Repairs & maintenance	65
Total Expenses	**$3,040**

NET INCOME FOR THE MONTH	$1,960

Sample 6-Months Cash Flow Worksheet

Month	1	2	3	4	5	6	Total
Starting Cash							
Cash Receipts							
Cash sales							
Layaways							
Credit card receipts							
Debit card receipts							
Total							
Cash Disbursements							
Start-up Costs							
Advertising							
Bank Charges							
Fees & Dues							
Fixed Assets							
Insurance							
Loans-Principal							
Loans-Interest							
Licenses & Taxes							
Purchases for resale							
Office supplies							
Professional fees							
Rent							
Repair & Maintenance							
Telephone & Internet							
Utilities							
Wages & Benefits							
Owner's Draw							
Monthly Surplus or Deficit (Cash less Disbursements)							
To Date Surplus or Deficit*							

* Monthly surplus/deficit to date is calculated by carrying through any deficit or surplus from month to month.

Accounts Payable/Receivable Reports

Accounts payable are those accounts that you must pay — the money or bills your store owes. Accounts receivable are any accounts that are owed your store — the money that others owe you. Accounts receivable reports can vary widely depending on how you do business. For instance, accepting credit cards or selling over the Internet will affect how this report looks. And you may sell more at certain times than at others. If you have a layaway plan, this will affect your accounts receivable as well.

Accounts payable reports will tell you what bills you owe and when they are due. It's important to know clearly what you owe before you make any additional purchases. You have to be able to pay all your incoming bills and still have enough money for the other things you need to purchase for your business. An accounts payable report will help you to schedule when you will pay your bills, and will help you make sure nothing is neglected or forgotten.

Balance Sheet

A good metaphor for a balance sheet is that it is a snapshot, like a photograph, of your business taken at one moment in time. A balance sheet is the quickest way to see how your store is doing at a glance. It shows you what you own and what you owe. In other words, it is a balance of your assets against your liabilities.

The balance sheet consists of:

- Assets (the items you own including your inventory)

- Liabilities (what you owe)

- Owner's Equity (what you've put into the business)

Types of assets are current assets and fixed assets (long-term and capital assets). A current asset is something that is acquired by your business over your business's fiscal year and will probably be used during that period to generate more revenue. Inventory, prepaid expenses such as rent already paid, and accounts receivable are examples of current assets. A fixed asset is an item that doesn't get used up quickly such as land, buildings, machinery, vehicles, long-term investments, etc., whose value is depreciated over time.

There are two types of liabilities: current and long-term. A current liability includes all those bills waiting for you to send a check out, such as utilities, short-term loans, or anything else payable within twelve months. A long-term liability is something that will be paid over a period of time longer than twelve months, for instance, a mortgage, a long-term equipment lease, or a long-term loan.

Owner's equity is anything you've personally contributed to (invested in) the business or any profit that remains in the owner's account that you have not drawn out in wages for yourself. If you used money from your personal accounts, or put your own assets into the business's inventory, the business "owes" you and it is recorded in this section of the balance sheet.

On the next page is what a typical balance sheet will look like. Note that assets balances exactly against liabilities + owner's equity. Also note that owner's equity equals assets minus liabilities.

5.5.3   Building Wealth

The following excellent advice on building wealth is adapted from the *FabJob Guide to Become a Coffee House Owner*, by Tom Hennessy.

Sometimes we get lost in the adventure of building a business and forget that on top of the perks of being our own boss, we can also make money in our venture. However, like all things, success doesn't just happen— you have to create it.

Even when you are making a good net profit each month, if you don't have a system for managing that profit, it can leak out during the course of a year. Then you will have nothing to show for your labor come New Year's Eve. In order to build wealth, you need to know how to squeeze all the value out of each and every dollar through budgeting, saving and investing.

Through these practices, you can build up a substantial amount of money without having a huge business. That is because time goes by very quickly. Five or ten years can slip away fast, and if you have a plan to carry you through those years, you will be amply rewarded. The two magic ingredients of time and compound interest are very valuable allies indeed.

Sample Balance Sheet

Balance Sheet [Company Name]
As of June 30, 20__

ASSETS	
CURRENT ASSETS	
Cash	$12,200
Accounts Receivable	1,000
Inventory	80,000
Total current assets	**$93,200**
FIXED ASSETS	
Furniture	$3,500
Vehicle	20,000
Total fixed assets	**$23,500**
TOTAL ASSETS	**$116,700**

LIABILITIES	
CURRENT LIABILITIES	
Accounts Payable	$5,000
Taxes Payable	2,225
Loan (short-term)	12,500
Current Portion of long-term debt	667
Total current liabilities	**$20,392**
LONG-TERM LIABILITIES	
Loan	$35,000
TOTAL LIABILITIES	**$55,392**

OWNER'S EQUITY	
Capital – Owner's deposits	$90,000
Less Owner's withdrawals	(32,500)
Net Income/Loss	3,808
TOTAL OWNER'S EQUITY	**$61,308**

TOTAL LIABILITIES & OWNER'S EQUITY	**$116,700**

Compound Interest and Debt

Think of compound interest as a steep hill. People are either on one side of this hill or the other. On one side of the hill, you have compound interest that you pay. On the other side is compound interest that is paid to you.

When you first start out in business, you generate a lot of debt. Your $200,000 loan may seem like a deal at 9 percent over 7 years, but is it really? By the time you pay off the loan, you will have paid an additional $70,295 in interest. That's over 35% of your loan.

When you are paying off your loan, you are looking up from the bottom of a steep slope towards the debt-free top. Most of the monthly payment is interest—hence the steepness. During the first year of the note, you have paid $21,486 in principal and $17,128 in interest. That is a lot of interest compared to principal.

By the end of the note, this ratio will level off. In the final year, you will pay $36,795 in principal and only $1,818 in interest. At the top of the hill, you are debt free. You owe no interest and you receive no interest.

A business can't really move to the other side of the hill and receive interest because the government punishes businesses that retain profits by taxing them. You need to spend money on capital improvements or pay it out in wages or other forms of compensation, again triggering taxes. A good accountant will help you to minimize paying taxes while maximizing compensation.

Paying Off Debt

Accountants don't like businesses to pay off debt too fast because it creates phantom income. This is because you can only expense interest, not principal since you never really owned the principal in the first place. It wasn't your money; you borrowed it.

When you wrote that loan payment check every month, the principal you paid back wasn't yours in the first place so it is not considered a legitimate expense. Only the interest that you pay on that loan payment is considered yours and therefore you are allowed to expense that portion of the payment.

In the example earlier, you paid $21,486 in principal and $17,128 in interest during your first year. You expense the interest on your income statement, but where does the principal go? You'll find it in the bottom line as profit. Only you gave that profit back to the lender and you get taxed on it, even though you don't actually have the cash anymore. That is why it is called phantom income. A good accountant can help you deal with this issue and at the same time help you to pay down your loan quicker and minimize taxes on phantom income.

If you can pay off your loan in 5 years instead of 7 years, you can save $21,197 in interest payments. That is significant. To generate the cash to do this, though, you need to learn the value of money.

Here is a good math lesson for you and your employees. Let's assume that you are netting 8% profit before taxes. Every time you spend money on expense items, that is money that normally would go straight to the bottom line in the form of net profit (except you spent it).

Suppose you bought a box of mechanical pencils for $9.95 at the office supply store. How much in the way of sales do you need in order to produce enough profit to pay for them? The easiest way to figure it out is to divide $9.95 by your net profit percentage, which is 8%.

$$\$9.95 \, / \, .08 = \$124.37$$

Looking at it another way, on $124.37 you would generate net profit of $9.95, which is 8% ($124.37 x .08). You need to sell an additional $124.37 in merchandise to produce enough profit to cover your pencil purchase. Every time you spend a dollar, a corresponding sale is needed to pay for it. That's over an above your regular sales. You'll need to generate an additional $124.37 above your usual sales in order to pay for your pencils.

Thinking about the value of a dollar in these terms can have a drastic effect on your bottom line. When you think about the amount of related sales needed to offset expenses, you'll consider your purchases more carefully.

Forced Savings Account

In a forced savings account, you automatically transfer a specific amount of money from your checking account into an interest-bearing account on a certain day of each month. It follows the old rule "Pay yourself first." If you don't do this, the year will slip by and you will have nothing to show at the end of it for all your efforts.

Even $100 a month is easy to do for most businesses. At the end of the year you will have $1,200 plus interest to do whatever you like with. Use it to pay for a vacation, employee bonus, or a new piece of equipment (that you didn't have to borrow the money for, saving even more money in paid interest).

Your bank can set this up for you. Your interest is better if your money is invested in treasury securities. Talk to a stockbroker or investment advisor about different options. For example, $2,000 per month invested in an index fund averaging 10% per year will grow to $412,227 in 10 years. At the same time, you want your money invested in something safe, but you want it to be accessible in case you need to write a check for some emergency.

There is nothing wrong with creating wealth. It is only through profit that you provide capital to grow your business and pay wages. You're taking responsibility for your own financial well being. As you save and invest, you start to live on the other side of the interest hill and you start earning money without actually having to work for it. It's a beautiful thing to watch.

5.6 Employees

"Hire good sales people who are cute and friendly. Educate your sales force, they need to know body shapes, dress cuts and materials. That way if a bride does not like a dress, your sales person can explain why and show her something that fits her better, so she does not get upset and leave."

— Haley Hughes, En Vogue Events, Houston, TX

5.6.1 When to Hire Help

Even if you plan to start on a shoestring budget, chances are you will need at least one other employee to help during busy times (weekends, especially), or to give you a day off here and there.

Many business owners prefer to work all the hours their store is open, closing shop a couple of days a week, during holidays and for vacations.

This system can work very well, especially if you notify your customers in advance of vacation time so they aren't disappointed with a wasted trip. You can even use the reminder as a selling tool by including a coupon for them to use when you return from vacation.

However, most shop owners reach a point in their careers where they want to make more profit by staying open more days or hours, or the store is so busy on a daily basis that they need the extra help at all times. In addition, malls and downtown business areas may have strict rules or bylaws about operating hours, and they'll fine you if you don't comply. You may not want to be in the store all the hours that it is required to be open, so you'll need to hire someone to be there when you're not.

Many retailers these days have a rule that if there are ever more than three people in line at the express checkout, then they will open another line. You might want to adopt this "three's a crowd" policy, too. If you consistently have more than three people waiting for help, or to make a purchase, then you may need to hire.

Take a look at your finances and make sure you can afford another employee. Are you making enough profit to hire extra help on the weekends and holidays? Will it increase your profits even more? If customers are getting frustrated at the wait time and leaving, then it most definitely will. Perhaps your business has even grown to the point where you need a full-time employee.

There are several types of staff members you can hire, and each has its advantages and disadvantages. All employees should be considered as investments, since you will spend time and money hiring and training them. You will see a return on that investment in increased sales, higher productivity in your store, more free time for you, and even new ideas for running your store based on employee input.

Full-time staff members work 30 or more hours a week. Most people work only one full-time job at a time, so, since they spend so much of their week working with you, they will naturally develop a sense of loyalty to you. In addition, full-time employees become so familiar with your store's routines and procedures that they can assist in training new staff members and run things if you need to take a day off here and there. A particularly competent and loyal full-timer might even become your second-in-command as manager when you take a vacation or open your second location. Keep in mind that full-time employees also come with the extra burdens for you of increased paperwork, health and other benefits, employment insurance, and so on.

Part-time staff members generally work less than 30 hours a week. Many people work more than one part-time job, often because of the unavailability in certain industries for full-time opportunities. (As discussed above, full-time employees cost more to employ.) As a result, loyalty will be less assured from your part-time staff and they are more likely to leave you if they receive a higher-paying or full-time job offer from another employer. However, the advantage to you is that you will save money, time and paperwork by hiring part-timers.

Students, retirees, stay-at-home parents, or people who otherwise have flexible or irregular schedules make good candidates for part-time work. All of these potential staffers typically welcome the chance to earn some income without the demand on their time that a full-time job would have. However, you may find that they require more training, since they may not have worked in the retail industry before.

Temporary, casual or on-call help can also play an important role as staffers in your business. For example, you might offer a particular service in your store that needs only occasional attention, so you hire someone who specializes in that type of service to come in once a week or twice a month to perform it. Another source of temporary help is your own family members, who might occasionally assist with sales or other tasks, particularly during peak busy periods like holidays.

No matter which type of employees you decide to hire, start small. Hire a part-timer to get a feel for being an employer. If you like the person you hired and they're working out well, you might want to offer them increased hours or even a full-time position. If you hire someone on a full-time basis in the beginning and find that you can't afford to keep them on full-time, you will likely loose that employee and generate hard feelings. Hiring someone part-time also gives you the flexibility to hire someone else if the person you originally hired doesn't work out.

5.6.2   Recruiting Staff

Hiring employees can be one of the most challenging aspects of owning a business. It can be difficult to find an employee who learns easily, is friendly with your customers, is honest, and comes to work on time.

Qualities of Great Employees

Have you ever gone into a store and been treated rudely or without concern by an employee? Everyone has run into a rude salesperson at some time or another. Sometimes store salespeople are so rude and so unconcerned that potential customers leave the store without buying something they fully intended to purchase. A rude employee can hurt your sales and cost you customers.

But if you pick the right employees, you will have other people who care about your store and the customers who come there, and who will work to make your store a success. So it is vital that you choose carefully.

As you think about the demands of your new store, the niche you are hoping to fill in your community and the customers you hope to have, make a list of the qualities you want in your employees. Think about the type of people who will be easy for you to work with, who will be warm and helpful to the customers, and who will be an asset to your store.

Consider some of the following qualities of great retail employees:

- Honest
- Hardworking
- Responsible
- Reliable
- Friendly
- Knowledgeable
- Polite
- Good sales ability
- Good customer service ability

- Niche experience (e.g. if you sell used clothing it is helpful to have employees with experience selling clothing)

Now that you know the kind of people you want, you have to find them. If you talk about your store — and you should, because it's a good way to generate excitement — you can ask everyone you come into contact with if they know someone who would be a good employee for your store. Your regular customers are a good source for referrals, and more than one store owner has hired a customer to work as an employee in their store. Almost everyone knows someone who is looking for a job — it never hurts to ask around.

Advertising

The first place to advertise your job openings is in your own store. You can put a "Help Wanted" sign in the front window, and another by the cash register.

Also consider placing an ad in your local paper's employment classifieds. Depending on the job market in your community, this can be an excellent way to find good local employees. Make sure your ad is eye-catching and uses just a few words to get the right kind of people through your door. Consider the following ad:

CAN DREAMS COME TRUE?
Busy bridal salon in Anytown Mall needs a bright, part-time sales associate to join our team. Are you fashion-savvy and great with customers? Do you love beautiful gowns? Retail clothing experience a plus. Great working environment. Please fax your resume to 555-1234 or call 555-1000 and ask for Bella Bryden.

Make sure the ad gets the point across quickly. Classified advertising is expensive and is priced by the word. Therefore, it is important to get your point across as quickly as you can. The ad above is about 50 words long.

Make sure all the vital information is included. Potential applicants need to know how to contact you or where to fax their resumes. Also, in order to save you lots of time with applicant questions, remember to include the basics about the job in your ad, including any benefits. One important thing to mention is whether the opportunity is full-time or part-time.

Make sure your ad is correct before it runs in the paper. When you work with an ad rep from your local paper, always ask them to give you a copy of your classified ad as it will appear, so you can check for mistakes. When your ad appears, check it again and make sure it is correct — especially your contact information.

Make sure that you include words or phrases that quickly help potential applicants find themselves in your ad. In the example advertisement above, the text includes the important words "gown" and "fashion-savvy." Potential applicants who have an eye for fashion and understand formalwear will know immediately that they should send you a resume, and the people who don't like weddings and don't appreciate fashion will know the job isn't for them.

When you run an ad, decide ahead of time if you are too busy for phone calls and would prefer the first round of submissions to be sent by fax or email. Taking prescreening phone calls from applicants is time consuming. Decide what works best for you and your hiring schedule.

5.6.3 The Hiring Process

The selection process starts with the prospective employee filling out an application. Here are some other things to look out for when prospective employees come in to fill out an application or drop off a resume:

- Are they dressed nicely? Well-groomed?

- Are they polite or do they say, "Gimme an application"?

- Are they alone? Chances are that if the potential employee can't come to fill out an application without their best friend, they can't work without their friends either.

- What does your gut instinct tell you?

The Interview Process

The purpose of an interview is to get to know potential applicants as much as you can in a short period of time. It is therefore important that most of that time be spent getting the applicants to talk about themselves. Most employers with limited interviewing experience spend too much time talking about the job or their store. And while that is certainly important, it won't help you figure out to whom you are talking and if that person is a good match for your store. A good rule of thumb to follow is that the applicant should do 80%of the talking.

To make the best use of your time, have a list of questions prepared in advance. This will keep the process consistent between applicants. You can always add questions that pop up based on their answers as you go along.

Possible questions to ask include:

- Why did you apply to work here?

- What is the ideal schedule you would like to work?

- When can you absolutely not work?

- What sort of experience do you have that you feel qualifies you for this job?

- Tell me about your last job and why you left.

- What was the best job you ever had-the one you had the most fun in?

- Who was your best boss and what made them so great?

- If I talked to someone who worked with you, what would they say about your work habits?

- Do you have any ambitions in this business? If not, what would be your perfect job?

To get a sense of how an employee will actually behave on the job, it is also a good idea to ask "behavioral questions." Behavioral questions ask applicants to give answers based on their past behavior. An example is "Tell me about a time you had to deal with a difficult customer. What was the situation and how did you handle it?" Instead of giving hypothetical answers of what someone would do in a particular situation, the applicant must give examples of what they actually have done. While people's behavior can change, past performance is a better indicator of someone's future behavior than hypothetical answers.

You can also ask questions that communicate your store policies to discover if the applicant will have any issues in these areas. Some examples are:

- When you are working, I expect your full attention to be on my customers. I do not allow private phone calls unless it is an emergency. Is that a problem?

- It is important that we open on time. I expect my workers to be punctual. Is there anything that could keep you from being on time for every shift?

By being clear on specifics and details in the interview, you can hash out any potential problems right then and there or agree to go your own ways because it is not going to work.

Discussing Pay

Another area to be clear about is what the pay is. Some employers will tell you not to talk money until you make the actual job offer, but that is really your choice. You do not want to go through the interview process, agonize over your decision, choose Johnny Good, offer the job and find out he does not want it because he thought it paid more and included health and dental benefits.

The government establishes a minimum wage that workers must be paid. Whether or not you want to pay over this amount is up to you. However, if you want the best candidates, then you'll need to offer them a competitive salary. Ask around — find out what other retail stores in your area are paying. To learn more about minimum wages in your area check out the U.S. Department of Labor website at **www.dol.gov/esa/minwage/america.htm**.

For wage information in a variety of occupations in Canada, visit the Service Canada website at **www.labourmarketinformation.ca** (click on "English", and then choose "Wages & Salaries" in the left frame menu). Visit **www.hrsdc.gc.ca/eng/labour/employment_standards** for Employment Standards in Canada, including information about minimum wage.

Ask your accountant to set up a payroll for your store and maintain it for you. That way, you can be assured that you are making the correct amount of deductions for taxes and other benefits.

Employees are paid either weekly, bi-weekly, or on the 15th and last day of each month. You should have sufficient funds in your business checking account to ensure payroll checks will be covered. You may offer employees direct deposit paychecks (in which their pay is deposited into their bank accounts) or regular checks (which they may take to the bank themselves).

References

Once you have found an applicant who appears to be a good fit, you can learn more by checking their references. The best references are former employers. (Former co-workers may be friends who will give glowing references no matter how well the employee performed.)

Many companies will not give you detailed information about a past employee. They are only required to give you employment dates and sometimes they will confirm salary. But many times you will be able to learn a lot about a potential applicant from a reference phone call. A good employee is often remembered fondly and even asked about by a former employer. An employer may not be able to tell you much about a bad employee for liability reasons, but they can answer the question "Is this employee eligible to be rehired?" Here are some other additional questions from Tom Hennessy, author of the *FabJob Guide to Become a Coffee House Owner*:

- How long did this person work for you (this establishes the accuracy of their applications)?

- How well did they get along with everyone (looking for team skills)?

- Did they take direction well (code words for "did they do their job")?

- Could they work independently (or did they sit around waiting to be told what to do next)?

- How did they handle stressful situations (this is important, especially if you are busy)?

If the references make you feel comfortable, call the employee to let them know they have a job and to come in and fill out the paperwork.

5.6.4   New Employees

After you shake hands and say, "The job is yours!", you have to know how to work with the new employee to make sure it is a positive experience for everyone.

New Employee Paperwork

When a new employee is hired there will be paperwork they must fill out. In the U.S. this will be a W-4 and an I-9 form. In Canada, the employee will give you their social insurance number; you must also have them fill out a TD1. The U.S. W-4 and Canadian TD1 are legal documents that will determine the amount of tax that is to be deducted from an employee's wages. The U.S. W-4 and Canadian T-4 forms are legal documents verifying how many tax deductions a new employee has. The amount of tax you will withhold as an employer varies based on the amount of deductions that an employee has. Have the employee fill out the forms, and then file them in a folder labeled with their name which you will keep on file.

Check with your state or province's labor office to make sure you are clear about all the forms employees must fill out to work. The sites below give more information on legal paperwork, including where to get blank copies of the forms your employees will need to fill out.

- *SmartLegalForms.com*
  (Sells blank forms online)
  www.hrlawinfo.com/index.asp

- *GovDocs Products - Employee Records and Personnel Forms*
  (Sells blank forms by the pack)
  www.hrdocs.com/Posters/hrproducts/

- *Human Resources and Skills Development Canada (HRSDC)* (Click on "A-Z Index", scroll down to "Forms Catalogue") **www.hrsdc.gc.ca/eng/home.shtml**

Employee Emergency Contact Card

If the unexpected happens, as it sometimes will, you want to be prepared. Having employees fill out an emergency card for their file will help you contact their doctor, spouse, or other friends or family members in case of an emergency. Besides being the most rational and human thing to do, being prepared in this way can safeguard you against liability.

Make sure every employee's emergency card contains the following:

- Their correct and updated address and phone number

- Their family doctor and choice of hospital

- Any medications taken

- Allergies or special medical conditions

- The name and phone number of a family member emergency contact

- The name and phone number of an alternate emergency contact

Make sure that the emergency cards for staff, including one for you, are filled out and placed in alphabetical order in a filing cabinet or another location, and that everyone who works with you knows where this information is kept. Ask employees to verify that their emergency information is correct and updated as soon as it changes.

New Employee Orientation

Showing up on the first day of a new job is stressful for any employee. The new employees you hire are full of hope and anxiety, and are trying their best to make a good impression and be successful in your eyes. You should do your best to make them feel welcome and appreciated. Here are some tips to help them succeed:

- Make definite orientation plans for your new employee. Develop a list of what you will show and tell your employee, and go through each point. (This is where it helps to have a procedures manual as described in section 5.1.)

- Plan for the employee to have lunch with you or a friendly co-worker on the first day.

- Don't expect your brand new employee to be able to do everything on the first day. Realize that the first few days in your store will be a time for your new employee to learn and become comfortable with procedures.

- Don't throw your new employee into the fire. Starting them out on the day of the biggest sale in your store's history is a bad idea. Choose a time that is relatively slow-paced to let your new employee learn in a calm environment.

- Once your employee has been working for a few days, schedule an informal meeting to check in. Ask them to voice questions, comments, and possible concerns. Offer some positive feedback about your new employee's performance.

Taking the time to make sure your new employee feels comfortable and positive working in your store will pay off in the long run. Happy employees who feel positive about what they are doing often become long-term assets for your business.

Training, Motivating, and Retaining

It costs less to retain the staff you have than to recruit and train new staff, so make sure you keep open lines of communication with your employees. Take the time to ask them how things are going. Listen intently to what they say. Perhaps they are spending more time in your shop than you are and can offer valuable insight to problems you might not have noticed.

Encourage, and if you can, pay for staff to take courses to help them be the best they can be at their jobs. This not only helps them feel good about themselves, but will solidify their attachment to you and your business.

Think of interesting ways to motivate your sales staff. Could you offer a discount on items? An incentive bonus for hitting a sales target? Find out what motivates them, and create a sales incentive program that suits them.

Commission-Only Personnel

If you decide that you're going to offer only a commission and not an hourly wage, bear in mind that this can lead to overbearing sales staff. However, a guaranteed wage might mean that as soon as you leave they whip out their favorite novel. Perhaps a mix of commission and guaranteed salary might work best for you.

Usually, commission-based sales staff receives between 15 to 20 percent of a sale, so you must factor that in to your selling prices. It's often best to pay bi-weekly, after the credit card charges and checks have cleared the bank. Commission is also subject to withholding taxes and vacation pay, so be sure to put it through your bookkeeping system correctly. If you have any questions, it's wise to call your accountant. Additionally, you might want to have a lawyer draw up a commissioned sales staff contract. It's always better to be clear at the outset before any miscommunications occur.

Don't forget that you will need to fill out all the required paperwork when you hire a new employee as discussed above.

Stay Informed

The government has many laws that protect workers in the workplace. It is important to be aware of these laws and to make sure that your store abides by them. The U.S. and Canadian governments have websites which provide information on almost any issue concerning employment law. Make sure to check how these laws affect your store and how you can abide by them. The U.S. Department of Labor website is located at **www.dol.gov**. In Canada, you'll find employment law information at the Human Resources and Skills Development Canada website at **www.hrsdc.gc.ca**.

6. Getting and Keeping Customers

6.1 Marketing Tools

6.1.1 Your Website

Your website is more than an electronic calling card. Many young women turn to the Internet to investigate purchases before they even consider making a phone call. According to Entrepreneur magazine, more than three-quarters of brides start their wedding planning online. With some savvy online marketing, you can make sure that potential customers find your bridal boutique when they're surfing the web.

Keep this in mind when you're building your website—offer plenty of information about your store's hours, about the gowns you carry (so be sure to include photos), and about any special services you offer. If a potential client likes your website, she's more likely to make a special trip to come in to your store.

Today, some brides also buy their gowns on the Internet. Brick-and-mortar bridal stores tend to frown on this practice, and not just because it means lost business. Because it's difficult for brides to know if the gowns they see online will fit properly, they can be sorely disappointed when the gown arrives and it's not right—which sours a bride's view of the whole gown sales industry. On your website, be sure to emphasize the importance of having personalized, custom fittings in your store, which will guarantee the bride's gown will fit perfectly on her wedding day.

Ideas for Your Website

The basic structure of your website should include the following:

- Home page to navigate through your site

- Categories pages (types of merchandise you sell), possibly with photos

- "About Us" page: this is where you let your customers know who you are and what expertise you have.

- Contact information with your store hours, address, phone number, fax number, and perhaps directions or a map

Here are some features and additional information to consider including on your own store's website:

- A photograph of the front of your store

- Information about parking around your store

- Gift certificate information

- Your email contact information

- Articles related to your business, such as product care tips or hot new trends

- Pictures of the latest gowns, or logos of their designers

- Testimonials from satisfied customers

- An online forum where brides can solicit input on their gown choices from friends and family members far away

Developing Your Website

Brides will judge the quality of your business by what they see on your site. If you don't have the time or expertise to design a polished website yourself, you can have a professional web developer build and maintain your site. There is no shortage of web designers, so consult your local phone directory or search online for one in your area.

If you are already experienced at creating web pages, or learn quickly, you can design your website yourself using a program such as Adobe Dreamweaver or a free program like SeaMonkey (available at **www.seamonkey-project.org**). You may also use the website development tools offered by domain and hosting companies, described below.

To present a professional image and make your web address easier for clients to remember, consider getting your own domain name, such as www.yourstorename.com. There are a number of sites where you can search for and register a domain name. One web host we have found that provides good service for a low cost is **www.godaddy.com**. Microsoft also offers a quick search for domain name availability using their sign-up feature at **http://smallbusiness.officelive.com**. (They'll also help you to set up a free website for your business.)

If your preferred domain name is available, but you're not yet ready with your website, you can also "park" your domain. This means that you register the domain so that someone else does not take it before you're up and running with your business website. You then park the domain with your web host.

Once you register your domain, you will need to find a place to "host" it. You can host it with the same company where you've registered the name. For example, if you register a domain name through GoDaddy, you might use their hosting services to put your website online.

You may also be able to put up free web pages through your Internet Service Provider (the company that gives you access to the Internet). However, if you want to use your own domain name, you'll likely need to pay for hosting. Yahoo! also offers a popular low-cost web hosting service at **http://smallbusiness.yahoo.com/webhosting/**. You can find a wide variety of other companies that provide hosting services by doing an online search.

Photography for Your Website

You can purchase low-cost photos (a few dollars each) through websites such as **www.istockphoto.com** or **www.dreamstime.com**. These sites are good sources for general bridal photos.

To show your store's merchandise, you may be able to use photographs supplied by the manufacturers. If you have other items that you want to take photos of, digital cameras allow you to take a picture and upload it immediately to your computer. The camera will come with detailed instructions on how to upload pictures for that specific model. Prices on these cameras have lowered considerably in the last few years and you can purchase a decent model for around $150. Check out product reviews at CNET for comparisons between models and prices.

- *CNET Reviews*
  (Click on "Digital Cameras".)
  http://reviews.cnet.com/

- *Consumer Reports*
  (Click on "Digital Cameras and Photography" in "Electronics".)
  www.consumerreports.org/cro/index.htm

If you already own a non-digital camera and a scanner, you can use this method to take photographs. Take the picture and develop as normal, then place the photograph on your scanner and upload to your computer according to your scanner's manufacturer's instructions. Points to consider for photographs on your website:

Make sure the subject is well lit but not washed out and not under-exposed. Often, taking the shot in the daylight is your best bet. You might find the need to buy a box for photographing small merchandise in order to make your pictures look their best.

You only need images of 72 dpi (dots per inch) for the web as opposed to the higher resolutions needed for printing of 260 to 300 dpi. It's important that, if you intend to use the same pictures for a brochure or any printed item, you shoot the picture at the highest resolution possible. Failing to do so will mean grainy printed pictures and an overloaded website.

Promoting Your Website

"To help launch our site, we sent an email to friends, family, people in the wedding industry, and everyone in our address books and asked them to forward it on. We received a great response and instant site traffic. Viral marketing truly works, and it's cheap!"

> — Susan Alexander Shapiro, founder,
> BravoBride, Seattle, WA

A great site is only as good as how many people it attracts. No matter how much you spend on making it beautiful, if people don't know you exist, it won't help you sell your store or its merchandise.

You will also want to establish a presence on wedding-related websites so that your boutique's name will come up in a bride's initial search. The two most popular wedding websites are WeddingChannel.com (2.4 million unique visitors each month) and TheKnot.com (2.1 million unique visitors each month).

These sites offer a range of advertising options. For bridal boutiques, the most cost-effective advertising choice is in the local service directory sections. The cost of advertising in these directories starts at $30 per month. See the Advertising section of these websites for more information about options and rates. The pages are **http://wedding.weddingchannel.com/about_us/article_1317.asp** for Wedding Channel.com and **www.theknot.com/wp_cityadsales.html** for TheKnot.com.

While some sites and search engines charge a fee to guarantee that your website will be included in their directory, you can submit your website for free to Google at **www.google.com/submityourcontent**. Once you're on Google, your site is likely to be found by other search engines as well.

Your web hosting company may offer a search engine submission service for an additional fee. You can find information about "optimizing" your website, to help it rank higher on search engines, at the Search Engine Watch website at **http://searchenginewatch.com** and at Google's Webmaster Help Center at **www.google.com/support/webmasters**.

In addition to the free search engine listings, you can use "pay-per-click" advertising to attract prospective clients. This involves paying for every visitor that a search engine sends to your website. You can find information about using pay-per-click advertising on Google, including how to target Internet users in your city, at **https://adwords.google.com/select/Login**. Other sites you can advertise on include Yahoo!, MSN.com, and Ask.com.

If you choose specific search terms that few other advertisers have bid on, you may be able to attract some visitors to your website for as little as five cents each. However, pay-per-click costs can add up quickly and some of the people clicking on your ads may simply be curious (for example, students doing research) and not serious prospects for your business. So you should set a maximum dollar amount per day and monitor your results to determine if this type of advertising is effective for you.

In addition to online promotion, make certain you list your site on all your business forms, cards, brochures, signs, and even your car, van or truck. Encourage people to visit your site by mentioning it as often as you can, for example, whenever you write an article, give a presentation, or are interviewed by the media. If you have items for sale on any other website, like eBay, add your website address. If you spend time on blogs (web logs) or newsgroups, add your site's hyperlink to your signature.

Finally, consider creating an email newsletter which your customers and visitors to your website can sign up to receive. Your newsletter could include articles about the types of products you sell and information about holiday specials, store events, and other news). One popular newsletter distribution service is Constant Contact which you can learn about at **www.constantcontact.com**. The cost starts at $15 per month for a list of up to 500 people, and a free trial is available.

Selling Online

While most of the customers who visit your website will come into your store to purchase their gowns and accessories, you may make some sales to wedding party members who live out of town.

You may also decide to sell some products online through a site like eBay, which is used by millions of buyers a day. Although eBay is the most well known, there are a variety of sites where you can list your products for sale. The most popular are:

- *Amazon.com Marketplace*
  www.amazon.com/gp/seller/sell-your-stuff.html/

- *eBay*
  www.ebay.com

- *Etsy*
  (For hand-made items.)
  http://www.etsy.com/how_selling_works.php

If you have not sold anything at one of these sites before, you can refer to the helpful free advice they offer for new sellers. For example, here is the link to eBay's very useful help pages and discussion forums where you can get advice from other users:

- *eBay Help*
  http://pages.ebay.com/help/index.html

- *eBay Community: Discussion Boards*
  http://forums.ebay.com

While these sites are not an effective way to sell new bridal apparel (most buyers are looking for deep discounts on used merchandise, and most brides need to try on a wedding gown before buying), you may be able to clear out items or sell accessories such as jewelry.

To sell online, you'll need a method of photographing your products as described above (sellers who include photos with their listings have more sales). When you create your item listing, it is best to place a photograph near the top of the page and describe the item thoroughly. Post your photographs, with several views and a few close-up details. Include information about the size, material, price, and whether you can alter the dress to fit other sizes. Include as much information as necessary to prevent any misunderstandings.

Be sure to spell out how much shipping will cost the buyer and when the item will be shipped. You may also want to make it clear what types of payment you will and will not accept and when it is due. A good rule of thumb is for the buyer to submit payment within two weeks of the closing date of the auction. For assistance with calculating various shipping costs visit:

- *The United States Postal Service*
  http://postcalc.usps.gov

- *Canada Post*
  (Click on "Rates and Prices")
  www.canadapost.com

6.1.2   Printed Materials

When you start your bridal salon business you will have to invest in some printed materials. These materials should be designed to promote the style of your bridal salon and attract customers to your store. Fonts on business cards, letterhead, ink colors, and even your advertising should all be designed to reinforce that style.

If you have a computer with a high quality laser or ink jet printer, you may be able to inexpensively print professional looking materials from your own computer. Free templates for all the print materials you are likely to need in your business can be found online.

HP offers templates for a variety of programs at **www.hp.com/sbso/ productivity/office**. For example, you can create a matching set of stationery (business cards, letterhead, envelopes) in Microsoft Word or a presentation in PowerPoint. The site includes free online classes and how-to guides to help you design your own marketing materials.

Another excellent resource is the Microsoft Office Online Templates Homepage at **http://office.microsoft.com/en-us/templates**. At this site you can search a database to find templates for:

- Business stationery (envelopes, faxes, labels, letters, memos, etc.)

- Marketing materials (brochures, flyers, newsletters, postcards, etc.)

- Other business documents (expense reports, invoices, receipts, time sheets, etc.)

As an alternative to printing materials yourself, consider using a company that provides printing services. You can use a local print shop, or your printed materials can be easily designed, paid for and delivered without leaving the house. Here are links to some companies that provide printing services for small businesses:

- *FedEx Office*
  www.fedex.com/us/office/copyprint/online/

- *Acecomp Plus – Printing Solutions*
  www.acecomp.com/printing.asp

- *The Paper Mill Store*
  www.thepapermillstore.com

- *VistaPrint*
  www.vistaprint.com

While the resources listed above can help with all your printing needs, here is some advice about two types of materials that are particularly important for marketing purposes – business cards and brochures.

Business Cards

Business cards are a must in any business. A business card gives customers the essential contact information for your store; every time you hand one out you should think of it as a mini-advertisement.

The cost of business cards can vary depending on how much or how little of the work you do creating them. You can make your own business cards if you own or have access to a computer with a printer. Office supply stores sell sheets of cards that can go through your printer.

You can also hire a graphic artist to design a logo, do the layout and even arrange for printing with a print shop. Most print shops have a design specialist on staff to help with these facets as well. When ordering your cards from a print shop, the more you order the less expensive they are. When you order 500 cards, for example, the cost is minimal, generally around $50 to $65 depending on how many colors you have on your card and the card stock you use. Shop around to see where you can get the best deal.

Another alternative when you're just starting out is to use free or low-cost business cards from VistaPrint.com. You can order 250 cards from them, choosing from a variety of contemporary designs, and you only pay for shipping. The only catch is that they print their company logo on the back. If you don't mind having their logo on the back of your business cards, this is very economical. If you prefer not to have another company's name printed on the back of your business cards you can order 250 cards for about $20 plus shipping from VistaPrint without their logo.

Brochures

An attractive brochure can be a helpful marketing tool, especially when you attend local events such as bridal fairs. Your brochure can communicate the most important information you have on your website (see section 6.1.1.).

When you have your written content and an overall look planned out for your brochure, take it to a graphic designer. If you don't have a graphic designer, any full-service print shop can help you with design. Expect to pay a minimum of $50 an hour for professional design and several hundred dollars or more to have your brochure professionally printed. Some print shops include design work free of cost when you print a certain quantity with them.

Many printers will have an in-house design department who can do the artwork for you, but make sure you have a hand in developing the text. You are the best-qualified person to describe what your business is all about. Also, check for any typos in your phone number, address or other contact information or you will be paying the printer to fix 1,000 brochures or doing it by hand.

If your budget is limited, you can use software such as Microsoft Publisher to design and print your own brochures, or you could try a free online brochure-making template where you create the design and print using your printer, such as HP Business Templates (**www.hp.com/sbso/productivity/office/brochure.html**). For a truly professional look you should enlist a service such as VistaPrint or a printer in your area to do it for you. Look in the Yellow Pages under "Printers."

While the challenge of designing an effective brochure is one thing, how to effectively distribute them is another. You should of course distribute them through your own salon. Your customers may take them away, share them with friends, and leave them where others can read about your salon.

In addition to your own salon, try to find other places to leave them where people might appreciate knowing about your salon. You might offer to carry the brochures of a complementary business, such as a hair salon or florist, in exchange for that business making your brochures available to their customers. Brochures can also be distributed by mail, handed out at events, and included as part of any packages you prepare.

Flyers

Flyers are essentially a brochure without the fold. They can be colorful and contain graphics, but often do not, making them more cost effective. A print shop will charge very little for 250 flyers with black print on colored paper, and you have the option to create flyers at home with a decent printer.

Many of the tips mentioned for creating an effective brochure apply to flyers. Again, pay special attention to your contact information and make sure that it is correct. Flyers can be handed out wherever brochures are distributed. You may also be able to post them on public bulletin boards. Depending on the community, you may be able to post your flyers at public libraries, college campuses, grocery stores, bookstores, and other public places.

6.2 Marketing Techniques

Assuming you have a good location, you will get some foot traffic off the street. People will walk into your bridal salon out of curiosity and some of them will buy from you. While this walk-in business can certainly contribute to your success, you can achieve even greater success by attracting customers to your store through effective marketing.

If your salon is located in a shopping mall, the mall administration will have a calendar of promotional events that you can participate in.

Likewise, if you have a store in a popular shopping district, there will likely be a local merchants association that you can join for cooperative advertising and events. In addition to any marketing you do through your mall or merchants association, you will likely need to do additional promotion on your own. This section outlines a variety of techniques you can try.

6.2.1 Advertising

A popular quote attributed to P.T. Barnum says, "A terrible thing happens when you don't advertise ... Nothing." In fact, advertising – paying for placement in the media – is essential for most retail businesses.

Media to consider for advertising your store include the Yellow Pages, newspapers, magazines, radio, television, and online. It's wise to try out a variety of advertising options to find what works best for you. However, advertising can be expensive, so make sure you thoroughly investigate the costs and audience of any media where you are considering advertising.

You can find this information by contacting media outlets and asking to speak with a sales representative. They will be able to provide you with either a printed or online "rate card" which includes information on the types of advertising they offer (such as size of ads in print publications), costs, and information about their audience (statistical information about their readers, viewers, or listeners). This information will help you determine if their audience is the sort of customers you are looking for and if it is the right media for your ad.

Yellow Pages

Yellow Pages ads can help you attract people from outside of your immediate area, particularly if you have a unique niche. Take a look at Yellow Pages ads for other retail stores like yours to get ideas (look under categories that match your type of business).

You can either design the ad yourself, have the Yellow Pages design it for you, or hire a designer. If you are interested in advertising, contact your local Yellow Pages to speak with a sales rep. Check the print version of your phone book for contact information. To find the Yellow

Pages online, go to **www.yellowpages.com** (U.S.) or **www.yellowpages. ca** (Canada).

Newspapers and Magazines

Many local newspapers and city magazines offer their readers an annual "bridal guide," usually in January or February. This is a special section of advertorial (advertisements written to resemble news stories), photographs and advertisements from wedding-related businesses. These kinds of special advertising guides usually have slightly better rates than the regular newspaper rates, as they're meant to draw in your advertising business.

Remember that all the bridal shops in town will be invited to participate in such a supplement (although whether they choose to or not is up to them). You can make sure your ad stands out by asking for "right hand placement" to ensure your ad appears on right-hand page or "exclusive placement" to ensure your ad is not on the same page as another bridal salon's ad.

Other newspaper advertising options are to purchase an ad in the section that runs local wedding announcements. Many brides-to-be read these announcements regularly, looking for ideas for their own upcoming nuptials. You can also contact the Lifestyle section editor of a daily to obtain a calendar of what wedding-related features are planned.

In addition to daily and weekly newspapers in your community, consider specialty magazines for your area that pertain to your store's niche. Read a magazine or newspaper carefully to see if an advertisement for your store would fit with the theme of the publication, the articles, and the other ads.

Nationally distributed magazines like Wedding Bells, Brides and Martha Stewart Weddings have extremely high advertising rates. Some wholesalers and manufacturers, however, advertise in these publications with a list of regional stores where readers can find their merchandise. If you are considering carrying a manufacturer's merchandise, ask them if they do this kind of "co-op" advertising. You'll typically pay a small portion of the overall ad cost to have your store's name included in the ad's list of authorized or selected retailers.

Advertising in national bridal magazines can be prohibitively expensive for a small bridal boutique. You wouldn't really be reaching your local target market, anyway. A better bang-for-for-the-buck can be found with local editions of the wedding magazines mentioned earlier. Wedding Channel and The Knot also publish local-edition magazines.

Also consider advertising in newspapers with classified ads for merchandise like yours. These might be known locally as a bargain, trader, or shopper newspaper. For example, one major advertising newspaper in the U.S. is **www.traderonline.com**, and a similar paper in Canada is **www.buysell.com**.

Some publications will design your ad for free, while others will design it for an additional cost and give you a copy of the ad that you can then run in other publications if you wish.

Creating Effective Ads

Some people spend years learning how to create the most effective ads. Since we do not have years, we're going to focus on a couple of key points. For additional tips on creating effective ads read the article entitled "How to Run Effective Advertisements" at **www.usatoday.com/small/ask/2001-07-30-ask-ad.htm**.

Most people need to see an advertisement several times before they buy, so running an ad only once may not give you as much business as you hope. A small ad that you run every week for a couple of months can generate more business than a single full page ad.

You can test a variety of ads, relatively inexpensively, by buying local ads on Google at **http://adwords.google.com**. Try different offers and wording to see which ones are most effective. You can set a maximum daily spending limit which keeps your costs down if lots of people click on your ad without buying. The offers that result in sales might also be effective in your other advertising as well.

One of the most effective ways to draw people into your store – and to test the effectiveness of each ad – is with some sort of incentive. An incentive can be anything from a discount coupon to a free gift.

The coupon should offer something that will motivate customers to take action they might not otherwise take – i.e. to come into your store. Some examples of offers that retailers have found effective are:

- buy one, get one free (sometimes called a "BOGO offer")
- (Click on "Business", then on "Rates & Prices".)
- a free item

Make sure the coupon has an expiry date printed on it, such as the last day of the month or people may put off using it. It should also requires customers to come into your store or visit your website to take advantage of the offer. By coming into your store or visiting your website, they may find other items to buy, and what started as someone simply planning to redeem a coupon for a free gift might result in a new lifelong customer for you.

Free gift items might include key chains, fridge magnets, pens, or other promotional items with your store name on them. You can find companies that provide promotional products by checking the Yellow Pages or doing an online search for "advertising specialties."

6.2.2   Free Publicity

One of the best ways to market — with potentially excellent results for minimal cost — is to get free media publicity. While you don't have the final say over what gets reported, the exposure can give a boost to your business.

Public Service Announcements

If you are working with a charity, you may be able to get a Public Service Announcement aired on local radio stations. Write a 15 second or 30 second announcement and send it to "Public Service Announcements" at local radio stations. It probably will not be prime time, during the drive home, but every bit of exposure helps. Also, contact your local cable company to find out how to submit Public Service Announcements to the community channel.

Press Releases

Another way to get free publicity in local newspapers or magazines is by using a press release. Press releases typically announce an event. They should be a page or less, encompass the main points, and be put together as though they were going to be printed verbatim in the newspaper (they sometimes are). A sample press release appears below. You can find additional tips at **www.publicityinsider.com/release.asp** and **www.xpresspress.com/PRnotes.html**.

While you can self-promote, you do need to tie it into the community somehow. Try to brainstorm ways your activity benefits the community. If you donate to charity, then this should be an easy tie-in for you.

Sample Media Release

FOR IMMEDIATE RELEASE   Date: April 16, 2010

CONTACT:
Bella Bryden, Owner
Something Old, Something New Bridal Salon
1234 State Street,
Everville, CA 99999
(555) 555-1234

Something Old Becomes Something New
for Cityside School Prom

Prom season will be a little bit more fabulous this year for more than 100 girls at the Cityside High School in downtown Everville, thanks to Bella Bryden and Something Old, Something New Bridal Salon.

Bryden, who has owned her wedding specialty store for just six months, is aiming to collect more than 100 gently used prom dresses for the girls at Cityside, which serves students from some of Everville's poorest neighborhoods.

"I got the idea when a girl came in to buy a dress not just for herself, but also one for her friend, who couldn't afford one," says

---

Bryden, herself an alumna of Cityside High. "I thought of all the Cityside girls who could benefit from donated dresses and set out to collect enough frocks for everyone."

Anyone with a gently used formalwear dress can donate it at Something Old, Something New now through May 15, from 11:00 a.m. until 7:00 p.m. Monday through Saturday. Bryden and her staff will host a "gown day" at the Cityside High gymnasium on Saturday, May 9.

Bryden opened Something Old, Something New Bridal Salon last September, following many years of charity work at a variety of local organizations.

"I was lucky to have had a beautiful prom dress when I was a teen, and I know how much it can mean," Bryden said. "This is my chance to help others."

Something Old, Something New Bridal Salon specializes in new and gently used wedding and formal wear, and is located in the Northside Mall on State Street.

For more information, contact Bella Bryden, 555-555-1234.

6.2.3 Donations

TIP: Connect with a charity and offer a regular benefit to that charity, or become known as a company that does good works.

"BravoBride is an online bridal salon where brides, newlyweds and bridal boutiques buy and sell new and gently used wedding items. That's an Earth-friendly and economical way of doing business everyone can feel good about. We're also supporting women's health because BravoBride donates a portion of the proceeds from each listing to the American Heart Association's Go Red for Women Foundation."

— Susan Alexander Shapiro, founder, BravoBride,
Seattle, WA

6.2.4   Networking and Referrals

One of the best ways to spread the word about your business is through other people. When you open your store, make sure you get the word out to your family and friends. Consider sending a postcard, and inviting them to your store's opening. You can also build your clientele by getting to know members of local clubs and by attending as many functions as possible to network with others who might help your business grow.

Chamber of Commerce

Often the local Chamber of Commerce and tourism groups are instrumental in getting the work out that you've opened a new business in town. Joining a group like the Chamber usually costs money, but the benefits, which include networking opportunities, educational seminars, and much more, is worth the investment for many business owners.

To find out how to contact your local Chamber, visit the national websites. For the U.S. Chamber of Commerce visit **www.uschamber.com/chambers/directory/default.htm**. For the Canadian Chamber of Commerce Directory visit **www.chamber.ca/index.php/en/links/C57**.

Word-of-Mouth

It's time to get your customers working for you. If you can get an emotional connection between you (that is, your business) and your customers they will be your best sales tools. What they say is worth more than hundreds of expensive ads.

One person telling another that your store is the best place to find wonderful merchandise is money in the bank. But how do you get to that point? By being everything your customers expect, honest, hardworking, fun to be around, knowledgeable, and—it's worth repeating—honest.

> **TIP:**   Ask special customers to write brief reviews of your store and services. Add these "testimonials" to your newsletter, brochures, and ads.

Get Referrals

One of the best ways to get referrals is to work with other complementary businesses. Put your fliers in their store and theirs in yours. Make a point of getting to know the florists, caterers, photographers and disc jockeys, as well as the wedding planners and coordinators in your area. As wedding industry professionals, you're all in the same boat, but with different services to offer. This means you can work together and offer each other referrals without fear of losing business to a competitor. You might also do promotions with them such as offering discounts to customers they refer to you.

As a new owner, building and maintaining relationships with other wedding vendors is the number one way to get your name out there and start building a positive reputation, say Keri Chantler and Jenni Hailer of Twirl Boutique, in Scottsdale AZ.

You can find also get referrals from your existing customers. To do this, get to know your customers by chatting with them when they're in your store. Don't be afraid to ask them if they know of anyone who could use your products and services, and ask them to refer that person to your store. You might also give a small gift or a discount coupon for bringing in a friend.

Of course, the best way to get your customers referring business to you from others is to offer them the best possible customer service. In section 6.4, we'll offer some customer service tips that will keep your customers happy and get them talking about your store to others.

> *"It takes time. You can do everything right, but be patient, just because you don't sell the biggest package, or most expensive dress in your first year that does not mean you are failing. Just breathe and keep going."*
>
> — Haley Hughes, En Vogue Events, Houston, TX

6.2.5   Other Marketing Ideas

There are a lot of even more unique ways to get the word out about your store. While you can and should use traditional methods of advertising, keep your mind open to new and exciting ideas as well, because you never know when you might stumble upon one that will be a huge success. Here are some additional ideas you may want to try to market your business:

- Hold a contest with an attractive prize. To be eligible for the prize, entrants should have to make an appointment for a bridal consultation or make a purchase in your boutique.

- Get your business card printed onto fridge magnets, or put your store information as pens, coffee mugs, or other items you can sell or give away. (Check online or your Yellow Pages to find companies that print promotional products.)

- Paint your shop logo on your car. If possible, include your web address, location, and a benefit of shopping at your salon.

- Contact your local Department of Motor Vehicles to get vanity license plates containing your store's name.

- If you don't have flyers, post your business card on every bulletin board you see.

- Offer specials such as 10 percent off one day a month to customers on your mailing list.

For bridal salons, some of the most effective marketing techniques involve organizing and participating in events, which are described in the next section.

6.3   Promotional Events

6.3.1   Your Grand Opening

One of the best ways to get people excited about your store is to hold special events. Some ideas for types of events and what you can offer include grand openings, fashion shows, and trunk sales.

Holding a grand opening can be a great way to introduce yourself and your new business to potential customers. If planned carefully, such an event can make your target market aware of your presence in a big way. The goal is to generate curiosity and interest in your business, as well as to make people aware of how you differ from the competition. If you're taking over an existing business you may want to let people know that the business is under new ownership and let them know how you plan to keep existing customers happy and serve the needs of new customers.

Some of the elements to consider when planning your grand opening are:

- *Budget:* how much money can you put toward the event?

- *Timing:* when is the best time to reach the most people?

- *Publicity:* how do you make people interested in attending your grand opening?

- *Invited guests:* who can help to attract people to your event (local celebrities, for example)?

- *Advertising:* what are the best ways to get the message out to your target market?

- *Promotions:* how will you reward people for attending?

Budget Considerations

There are a number of factors you should consider when planning your grand opening budget. First, you should put aside a certain amount of money in your start-up budget (see section 3.3 for more about start-up financial planning) for the event. Whether your start-up capital comes from your own cash resources or a loan, your plan for a grand opening should be clearly stated in your business planning documents.

Some grand opening budget items include extra staffing, advertising, printing invitations, brochure or flyers, buying promotional items, hiring a master of ceremonies, hiring a remote local radio broadcast from your store, hiring a guest speaker or celebrity look-alike, hiring a D.J. or band, hiring a caterer to supply refreshments, etc. You should find out the costs for all of these things well in advance and then figure out how much of your start-up cash you can devote to each.

Timing Considerations

When to hold your grand opening is also a major consideration. If you are in a downtown location, then the best time to hold your grand opening might be through the week when traffic is high in the area. If you are opening in a mall or strip mall, then the best time might be on the weekend when these are busiest.

Another consideration is the season. You shouldn't plan a grand opening close to any major holidays, since people are too busy to give much attention to a new store opening. Worse, many people travel during holiday times and this can have a negative impact, too.

Time of day is important, also. According to one Chamber of Commerce source, the best time of day for a grand opening is from Tuesday through Friday, from 10:00 a.m. to 12:00 p.m., because this is the best time to get media attention and maximize attendance. You can informally survey local businesses where you plan to open to determine the highest traffic periods in that area.

Publicity and Advertising Considerations

There are a number of ways to get publicity for your event. You might want to consider a press release; distributing brochures, flyers or menus; contacting your local radio or television station to ask them to do an interview with you; paying for a remote on-location broadcast and so on. Earlier sections in this chapter have great advice on how to generate publicity and tips for effective advertising.

Promotional Considerations

In promoting your grand opening, you'll want to give people a reason to attend. Put yourself in the place of your hoped-for clientele and answer for them the question: "What's in it for me if I attend?" The answer might be something like a 10-20% discount on products or services, a free sampling of your services, free refreshments (some businesses offer coffee and doughnuts or a barbecue), gift merchandise (giveaways) and so on. The chance to meet a highly regarded celebrity can also be an incentive.

Invited Guests

Who you invite to your grand opening can also have an impact on attendance. You might want to have the mayor or other high-profile citizen cut the ribbon to officially open your business. Perhaps you know someone famous who wouldn't mind helping out for the event.

Another consideration is to invite people who have a wide network of contacts. They can help to spread the word about your business. Other people to invite include:

- Local Chamber of Commerce members

- City or town council members

- Other government officials

- Local business owners

- Any contractors who worked on remodeling your store

- Business Improvement Area representatives and members

- Any other person or group who you know has a wide sphere of influence

6.3.2   Trunk Shows

Many gown designers and wholesalers offer trunk shows, in which they bring samples of their newest designs to your store to show to customers. These offer a good promotional opportunity because they provide a chance for customers to ask questions directly of the designer or their representative, and because some wholesalers will offer percentage discounts or special rates for any order placed during a trunk show.

When you hold a trunk show at your bridal salon, you'll be responsible for promoting it to local media and your clients. If you have a regular electronic mailing list of clients, make sure they're alerted. Give them at least two weeks' notice. For local media, two to three weeks' notice is good. Let them know what designer will be represented, and when the show is happening. If you can put a local journalist in touch with your wholesaler's representative in advance of the show, you may be able to get an article written about it.

At the show, it's considered courteous to remove or conceal your inventory of gowns made by designers other than the one giving the show, but this is not often practical. You should, however, provide a clear area of your store for your wholesaler to use as a display area and/or stage. Your wholesaler will help you determine how to set up the store in

A Sample Grand Opening Plan

Grand Opening Budget

Extra staff (4 hours)	$100.00
Master of Ceremonies	$500.00
Advertising Costs	$600.00
Printing Costs	$450.00
Catering service	$500.00
Balloons	$50.00
Ribbon	$30.00
Remote on-location radio broadcast	$500.00
Giveaways (at cost)	$200.00
Total Grand Opening Costs	**$2,930.00**

Schedule

9:00 a.m.	Meet with staff and go over the plan
9:15 a.m.	Start setting up, local radio crew to arrive to set up for on-location broadcast
9:30 a.m.	Caterer to arrive with refreshments
9:45 a.m.	Master of Ceremonies and Mayor to arrive
10:00 a.m.	Invited guests to arrive; greet guests and the public in front of the store
10:15 a.m.	Mayor to cut ribbon; invite guests and public inside
10:20 a.m.	Refreshments to be served
10:20-11:30 a.m.	Meet and greet; interviews with local radio talent
11:30-11:50 a.m.	Hold draws for door prizes
11:50 a.m.	Thank everyone for coming. Final words from M.C.
12:00 a.m.	Start clean-up

preparation, and will also let you know what kinds of space or accommodations they require. Expect to have extra staff on hand during a trunk show, both to handle client questions and sales, and to pay attention to security.

6.3.3   Bridal Expos

Bridal fairs or expos are yearly events sponsored by major bridal-related companies, including department stores, magazines, honeymoon hotel chains and others. You can either rent a booth at one of these events, or sponsor a prize such as a free gown (sponsorship usually includes a booth).

These shows are two to three days in duration, and can attract up to 10,000 visitors a day. One of the largest bridal expos is The Great Bridal Expo, which sponsors events in cities around the country. The link below will take you to their latest tour schedule. The other two links are to help you find other local bridal shows.

Participating in a local bridal expo is an excellent way to meet potential clients. At these events, you rent a booth where you can set up a display of your merchandise. Brides-to-be attend these events, often bringing their mothers or maids-of-honor, to see what's available for their upcoming weddings. An event like this is a chance to meet these potential clients, and to make an impression on them.

> Bridal expos will often have speakers discussing topics of interest to brides, and fashion shows to display the latest trends in wedding wear. Make sure to contact event organizers well in advance and let them know you'd like to participate in these features. Giving a talk or having some of your gowns included in the fashion show are both excellent ways to gain additional exposure.

Set up your booth in a way that reflects the style of your store. If you have a simple, elegant retail space, for example, do the same for your booth. Things to bring to your bridal expo booth:

- Gowns or other merchandise for display

- Mannequins, display hangers, display shelving

- Mirrors, if you have items that can be tried on right there

- Plain fabric to use as a backdrop (booths typically have uniform curtains and tablecloths, but you can customize if you bring your own)

- Brochures about your store

- Business cards

- Samples

- Promotional giveaways like logoed pens, mugs, etc.

- Cards on which brides can write their names and contact information, to be entered in a special prize draw. For the cost of one prize (whatever you choose to give away), you'll get the contact information of hundreds of possible clients.

- Small treats, like wrapped candies or chocolates

Find out about bridal expos in your area by visiting these websites:

- *The Great Bridal Expo*
  www.greatbridalexpo.com/tourschedule.aspx

- *Bridal Show Producers International*
  www.bspishows.com

- *Bridal Shows*
  www.weddingdetails.com/shows

6.3.4   Hold an Open House

Holding an open house is a good way to introduce customers to your merchandise in a casual, no-pressure way. They might not be ready to purchase a wedding gown yet, but it never hurts to let potential clients see what you have. They'll remember and dream about their favorite gowns, and return when it's time to buy.

Scheduling and Advertising Your Open House

Schedule your open house for a date and time when you know there will be plenty of parking in the parking area, and your whole staff is available to attend. Evenings and weekends are good for these reasons.

Plan your open house to last about two hours—long enough for lots of people to come, but short enough that there's always a crowd.

Advertise your open house in-store, on your website, with a big sign in your window, and in the newspaper or on local radio stations. It's a good idea, if you're participating in a bridal expo or a newspaper Bridal Guide, to hold your open house about a week after the event happens or advertisement runs, so that you can use these vehicles to invite potential clients to your open house.

Planning Activities for Your Open House

At the event, you'll basically open the doors to your shop and let clients examine, admire and try on merchandise. It helps to plan a few activities to keep clients' attention. Post a schedule where clients can see it, and stick to the schedule. You'll keep more people around for longer if they know it's only ten more minutes until the "how to wear a veil" demonstration.

Consider inviting a local florist to demonstrate different types of bouquets to complement your gowns, or a photographer to show clients the best ways to pose in their gowns. You can even give a brief talk about new styles and trends, especially if you've been to a recent bridal market and have exciting new products to show off.

Offer light refreshments, but keep in mind that refreshments bring the chance of spills or sticky fingers touching your merchandise. Choose "clean" finger treats like Jordan almonds (a traditional wedding favor) or provide toothpicks (and a disposal container) for people to use to spear snacks. And absolutely no red wine or juice! Stick to white wine, white grape juice, or sparkling mineral water to minimize stain potential.

Other Tips for a Successful Open House

You can offer special discounts for any orders placed/gowns purchased at your open house. You could offer to pick up the sales tax for that day only, give a percentage discount, or offer a giveaway add-on, like a free pair of shoes or earrings. If you do choose to give away an item, make sure you have enough in stock to prevent anyone being disappointed.

You can also hold an open house just for bridesmaids, or just for prom gowns, or even just for holiday formalwear. Plan these events to happen at least a month or two before the holidays or prom season, in order to catch clients before they've really begun to shop for their outfits.

6.4 Customer Service

"You have to love weddings, and be passionate about helping each bride's vision come to life. Understand that you are more than just a retailer selling dresses - you are a key element in making each of your brides have her perfect day. With that mind-set, not only will you sell more dresses, but you will create relationships with customers who depend on you."

> — Keri Chantler and Jenni Hailer, Twirl Boutique, Scottsdale AZ

Once you get those blushing brides into your store, the real work begins. According to the editors at Modern Bride magazine, most brides will visit four or five stores and try on 16 or 17 gowns before they find "the one". Therefore, to be successful in the bridal boutique business, you have to be able to close the deal. That means delivering great service and mastering the art of the bridal sale. It begins with how you greet customers.

6.4.1 Greeting Customers

"There's nothing worse than for a bride to walk into a salon and feel like they aren't wanted or noticed. ... The person who may come in with ratty looking Levis may have a pocket full of money to spend, and if they aren't treated well, will take it elsewhere."

> — Tanya W. Porter, author, owner of Weddings Etc. LLC, Englewood, CO

Most bridal boutiques prefer to book brides by appointment. This ensures that each customer will have your full attention and get the service she needs – and you will be able to address her by name.

Of course, if you've chosen your location well, you will probably also get customers walking in off the street to browse. There's no way of knowing for sure who's a serious customer and who's just looking. It's frustrating to waste your time. However, good service can convert a browser into a buyer. And making the wrong assumption is a good way to lose a potential customer.

Most customers behave similarly when they walk into a small retail store. First, they want a greeting just to know someone is there. Second, they might be cautious for the first few minutes, hoping no one will pounce on them with a high pressure sales pitch. To set customers at ease, you should keep the chit-chat light at first. They'll soon start to loosen up and then you could ask what they are looking for.

Consider using this three-step approach to greeting customers:

- *Step #1:* When customers enter the store, greet them. Say, "Hello. How are you?" Smile, smile, smile. Never, ever ignore your customers. Assume the store is like your home and the customers are your neighbors coming in for a visit.

- *Step #2:* Pause for a minute and then start some chit-chat. "Isn't it a beautiful day outside?" or "I like your necklace." Keep it positive and upbeat. Don't say, "Don't you hate this lousy weather we're having?"

- *Step #3:* Last, but not least, ask if they need help. "Can I help you look for something?" "Did you come in for something specific today or just browsing?"

Customers do not like feeling pressured. However, they also do not like feeling ignored. We've all been in stores where staff members are busy chatting and joking with each other and ignoring customers, or they're on the phone with a personal call, too busy to be disturbed by a customer. Even if your store is busy with several customers at once, make sure you at least acknowledge the person when they first come in and let them know that you're around to offer your help if needed.

Greeting Customers by Name

You will need a good memory to pull this one off, but writing down a description of the person and some details can jog your memory. You may not remember every single person who comes into your store, but you should make an effort to get to know the regulars and you should greet brides who have an appointment.

There are a few visualization techniques you can use to recall someone's name. There are a couple of articles you can read online that will help you with this skill. The first, "How to Remember Names" (**www.learnthat.com/courses/lifestyle/names**) is a short article that offers some easy memory devices like repetition and word association to use in order to remember names. The second, "How to Remember Names" at **http://ezinearticles.com/?How-To-Remember-Names&id=470003** is a little more in-depth, and expands on some of the concepts in the first article. In addition, the article introduces devices like mnemonics and "cluster imprinting" for recalling people's names.

> **TIP:** Another way to show customers they are important is to focus on them. If you are working with a customer and the phone rings, allow the machine to pick it up. You can return the call as soon as you are finished with the customer who is in the store.

6.4.2 Giving Brides What They Want

"Realize this is a very important day in someone's life and you can make a big difference for them."

— Eva D'Avella A Fairytale Wedding, Los Angeles

Start by creating an environment that's conducive to pleasant shopping. Provide roomy try-on areas and seating for the bride's shopping companions. Offering water to the bride and tea or coffee to the waiting guests is also a nice touch. Your boutique should smell pleasant, but not overwhelming, and convey a relaxed atmosphere to help the bride be herself. Organize your stock in a way that's easy to browse without the help of a consultant.

Of course, expert consultation is the service that sets a full-service bridal salon apart from discount bridal stores and department stores. Bridal salon staff should be true experts on the wedding industry. A trained bridal consultant should be able to show a bride options that she never would have found on her own. Here are some ways to offer exceptional service to brides:

- Listen. Most brides have specific ideas of what they're looking for.

- Know your products. Shopping for a bridal gown can be overwhelming. Your expertise can take a lot of the stress out of the process for your clients.

- Give tactful advice. If a customer asks your opinion about an unflattering gown, be diplomatic. If you think a different silhouette or style would look better on her, position it as a positive. Instead of telling her the sheath dress makes her hips look wide, tell her the A-line will showcase her lovely hourglass figure.

- Be patient. The average bride tries on many gowns in multiple stores before deciding.

- Practice the art of the up-sell. Put together a whole wedding-day look, complete with shoes and veil and jewelry. Accessories can make a beautiful gown look even better. If you do your job well, you may end up selling a complete wedding ensemble instead of just a dress.

- Be size-savvy. Wedding gowns run small, so brides should always order at least one size up from their normal dress size. Check the designer's sizing chart prior to ordering, and never let a bride or bridesmaid order a too-small size because she is planning to lose weight. It will only lead to heartache and hassles.

- Be on your best behavior. The Internet has created a whole new type of word of mouth. Wedding websites like WeddingChannel.com and TheKnot.com have very busy message boards where brides post complaints about bad wedding vendors and sing the praises of good ones. Treat every customer as if she will be posting an account of her experience for brides all over the world to read.

- Be a girlfriend if needed. Some brides are miles away from their mothers and bridesmaids, and are shopping for gowns on their own. Offer to help do up zippers, buttons and bustiers, and do your best to make them enjoy the solo experience.

6.4.3   Making the Sale

The key to making the sale is to find out what the customer wants, and have her feel that you can give her what she wants. To do that, you'll first need to get her to talk about what she is looking for. Ask questions that lead to a conversation, not just elicit a yes or no response.

Relationships of all types require work. Be very careful when you're subtly trying to find out what customers want and why they aren't buying that you don't overstep that line of comfort that most people need to keep salespeople at arm's length. They want to feel in control of the situation, and if you push too hard their discomfort will mount and they may run out the door. Some shoppers would rather browse in silence and you'll become quite adept at figuring out who they are the minute they walk into your store. They will be courteous, and return your greeting, but perhaps only smile tightly if you offer any further conversation.

How do you know if you've gone too far? Answers to your questions will become clipped; customers will avoid your eyes, and begin to move closer to the door. Re-establishing a level of trust might be quite difficult at this point, so it is probably best to be as friendly as possible, apologize, and offer them room to continue to look at their leisure.

TIP: Ask for the sale. Say, for example, "Can I wrap this up for you?" or "Will this be cash or charge?" You might get the odd customer who laughs and backs away quickly, but you'll soon find your own rhythm and know just when to head them over to the cash register.

Handling Common Objections

It's unlikely that the bride is going to love the first dress you bring out to her. If a customer has objections to buying, you need to listen carefully to why that person isn't buying. Are they looking for a different type of item or design than you're currently stocking? Hopefully you will be able to save the sale, but this might be a good time to scrutinize your inventory and prices to see if you need to make some changes. Here are some common objections you'll hear from clients on a daily basis, and how to interpret them to your advantage.

"It's too expensive."

Work with the bride to better understand her budget. Suggest lower-cost alternatives if available. If the bride is simply trying to maneuver you down on price, reassure her that your prices are as good as (if not better) than your competitors.

You may want to tactfully ask what the approximate budget for the wedding is. This way, you can point out to her that the price of the gown is a small fraction of what will be spent on the day in total. If she isn't happy with her dress, the money she spends on photos will be wasted, since she won't like how she looks in them.

Layaway Policy

Allowing a customer to layaway items is entirely up to you, but it is a great service to offer, and will ensure the customer returns several times to make payments and possibly purchase more in your store. Many retail stores offer layaway plans but usually only on items that are expensive. Remember that while they are paying for the item, it's costing you money to keep it on the floor or in storage in your back room.

If you decide to do layaway, make sure you give your customers a specific amount of time and a final date as to when you expect them to finish paying for the item. Put it in writing. You can write the date on the sales slip; you don't need an attorney to come up with a special form. Put on the slip when you expect incremental payments. Make sure everything is clearly spelled out.

Most shops will allow a customer to walk away from an item if they change their mind, but will not return the deposit that has been paid toward the item. Be clear about your store layaway policy and put it in writing.

"I like it, but I'm just not sure it's 'the one'."

Ask leading questions to determine what the bride's issues are with the gown, so you can identify what might be a better fit. Encourage her to try on additional dresses so she can feel confident she's looked at all alternatives. Sometimes it takes seeing a bunch of other dresses on to settle on the one she liked in the first place.

"It's perfect, except for the sleeves/neckline/beading/etc."

Bring out some similar dresses in your sample collection without the offending feature. You can also find out if the feature she doesn't like can be changed — many custom-dress manufacturers will agree to customize gowns.

"I saw a similar gown for much cheaper at the discount store/online/on eBay."

Point out the advantages to buying the gown in a full-service bridal boutique, such as on-site alterations or custom manufacturing. Note the quality of the merchandise (what she saw may be a cheap knock-off), any guarantees or refund policies offered, and your reputation as a reliable businessperson who delivers on promises. Ultimately it's up to them where they choose to shop, but with them in your store, you have the upper hand.

6.4.4   Return/Exchange Policy

For the most part, you are free to choose your own return and exchange policy. You may decide returns are not right for you because they create havoc with your bookkeeping. Or you may decide that the customer is always right and since you want them to come back to your store, you will work with them on the items they do not want.

It's up to you what returns policy you create, but remember a lot of people judge a shop by its returns policy. Perhaps you feel hanging the sign "Exchanges Only" is a fair policy, or perhaps you want to keep people happy no matter what and offer a no-questions-asked, money-back guarantee.

Many bridal salons do not offer returns or exchanges because most wedding gowns are custom-made for each client and have been carefully chosen and fit to a specific customer. However, try to be flexible. There may be exceptions to any rule you establish.

If you seem hard to deal with (your sign at the cash register screams, "All Sales Final!") you may end up with very unsatisfied customers.

Sometimes you will need to give customers their money back even if you think they're wrong or have abused your returns policy. It's always best to have a customer leave your store satisfied because an unsatisfied customer can be a word-of-mouth disaster for you.

Something else to keep in mind is that certain jurisdictions, usually under specific circumstances, have a "buyer's remorse" rule. This means that a customer has the right to change their mind about a purchase or contract, and back out of the sale within a specified time period (usually 10 days). You have no choice but to comply. Check for rules like this in your locality and retail sector before you implement a "No returns or exchanges" policy.

Think carefully about what kind of policy you want to speak for you.

Following is an example of a return and exchange policy:

Sample Return/Exchange Policy

[*Name of your store*] inspects all gowns upon arrival from the manufacturer, and therefore will not accept returns/exchanges due to defects in manufacturing. If, upon first fitting, you discover flaws in the gown's manufacturing, we will do our best to fix the situation.

- We do not accept returns or exchanges on custom orders.

- All returns/exchanges on off-the-rack merchandise must be accompanied by the original sales receipt and must be made within 24 hours of purchase. Original tags must still be on the garment. We do not accept any returns or exchanges on Saturdays or Sundays.

- Purchasing an item, using it, and then returning it is not an acceptable use of the return policy.

We want to work with you to make sure you are happy with your experience in our store. Come in during regular business hours to discuss any concerns with our friendly staff.

6.4.5   Getting Repeat Business

To maximize your sales, take a proactive approach to identify your customers and keep them coming back. A happy bride may return to your store to buy gowns for formal events, help her sister find a prom dress, or recommend your store to a friend who is getting married.

> *"Our most effective marketing tool is customer service. That may sound strange, but when tracking how new customers find out about Twirl, over 90% is word-of-mouth. When we first created Twirl, we assumed we were in a business that wouldn't see many repeat customers. As the years have gone by, though, we have former bridesmaids bringing in friends who are getting married, or coming back in because they are getting married themselves."*
>
> — Keri Chantler and Jenni Hailer, Twirl Boutique, Scottsdale AZ

Giving Customers What They Want

To give customers what they want, you need to know something about them. While the amount of customer information you keep in a customer database is entirely up to you, try to keep as much information as your software program allows.

Here are a few of the things you might want to keep track of:

- Customer preferences
- Buying patterns
- Special interests

You will probably at least want regular customers' mailing information and some of their preferences listed. Once you know your customers' interests and preferences, you can make suggestions.

Suggesting items that you think will suit the customer can show you're interested in the customer themselves — not just a sale. Take the time to work with your clients and find out what their needs and desires are. Ask your customers what they want, whether it's something you currently carry or not (you could even include a brief survey in your email newsletter). Then create a wish list in a note book and keep it up-to-date.

Once you have been in business for a while, you will have a few regular customers who shop from you year round. Pay attention to their likes and dislikes and track them. If you get something in that you know they would love, pick up the phone and give them a call. Again, this is excellent customer service. You will more than likely make additional sales as well, because they will likely buy several things while they're in picking up the new item that you have put aside for them. These extra touches and consultations can keep customers coming back again and again.

Paying special attention to bridesmaids and flower girls is a good practice, because in doing so, you're sowing the seeds for future customers. If a ten-year-old bridesmaid has a good experience in your store, you know that in a few years, she'll beg her mother to buy her prom dress there. And if she loves her prom dress, she's bound to return to your store again to find her perfect wedding gown.

Dealing with Difficult Customers

"Remember that you're dealing with people who are extremely emotional. Know that most of the time issues arise when clients feel like they're not receiving enough time or information. If you're waiting on answers from someone, relay that to your bride so that she doesn't think you're just not returning her call or e-mail."

— Keri Herndon-Brown,
Events By Keri, Atlanta, GA

One of the best ways to deal with difficult customers is to gather as much information as you can. Let's use an example. Perhaps you have a customer who consistently buys items and returns them. You suspect that they are using them and then bringing them back to get their money back, but you do not really have any proof of this.

The customer comes into your store once again with a return and you ask what was wrong with the item. Do not immediately close your ears because you think you know the answer. Really listen to what they have to say; practice those listening skills we just discussed.

Asking customers for feedback can help you determine what the real issue is (they may not be using the item at all) and this may help you further develop your store policies manual as discussed in section 5.1.

Customer Surveys

Feedback can also help you keep your good customers coming back. Each time a person buys an item, ask them to take the time to complete a survey, which will include the types of items they like to collect, or have an affinity for. Keep survey sheets near your cash register and also have a survey on your website. Be careful, though, because privacy laws are very specific, and you need to ensure you customers that you won't be sharing the information you collect and how you will be using it.

TIP: By offering an incentive, such as a prize (perhaps a gift certificate or discount coupon), you will find people are more inclined to fill out your survey. Let them know that this way, if you get something in they may love, they will be the first to know.

Sample Customer Survey

Name: _____

Address: _____

_____

Phone: _____

Email: _____

Any particular item(s) you are interested in acquiring? Please describe your wish list.

_____

_____

_____

_____

Can [Store Name] send you newsletters about events and special promotions?　❑ Yes　❑ No

Please note: [Store Name] will only use your information to provide better services to you; your information will not be shared.

Sorting through the contacts you make this way might seem time-consuming, but setting up a database, either by a simple listing in a spreadsheet, which you can sort and search, or using a database program, is the key to making sure you use the information you have taken the time to collect.

Set up your system to be able to search categories that match your customers' wish lists against new items you get in; for example, a simple category listing that then expands to the various types in that category that they are interested in.

You might want to rate which customers to contact first, perhaps by how well they pay or by how often they have been in the store. Let them know they are preferred customers.

Conclusion

Now that you have a good number of professional tips and tricks up your sleeve, you're well on your way to becoming a successful bridal salon owner. Imagine the satisfaction you'll feel when you sell your first gown—seeing the bride's eyes light up as she sees herself in the mirror for the first time, wearing the gown of her dreams that you helped her pick out, will be as exciting an experience for you as it will be for her.

Remember that a successful retail venture takes a lot of hard work, as well as support from a wide community of vendors, staff, and clients. There will be difficulties, but you can overcome them by keeping in mind the expert advice offered in this guide. And, just like a successful marriage, your bridal salon and the relationships you develop along the way will bring you joy and satisfaction for years to come.

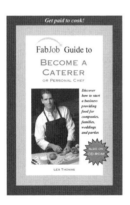

More Fabulous Books

Find out how to break into the "fab" job of your dreams with FabJob career guides. Each 2-in-1 set includes a print book and CD-ROM.

Get Paid to Plan Weddings

Imagine having an exciting career that lets you use your creativity to organize the happiest day of people's lives. The **FabJob Guide to Become a Wedding Planner** shows you how to:

- Plan a wedding ceremony and reception
- Select reputable vendors and avoid disasters
- Get a wedding planning job with a resort, tourist attraction or other wedding industry employer
- Start a wedding planning business, price your services, and find clients
- Plan your own wedding like a professional wedding planner
- Be certified as a professional wedding planner

Open Your Own Clothing Store

Do you love clothes? You may spend a lot of time in boutiques, but nothing compares to the fun and financial rewards of having your own store. The **FabJob Guide to Become a Boutique Owner** shows you:

- How to decide what type of boutique to open
- How to create a business plan and get financing
- Choosing a location (plus lease negotiation tips)
- Where to get merchandise for your boutique and how to set your prices
- Important advice for managing your boutique business (from hiring staff to preventing theft)
- How to attract customers and increase sales

Visit www.FabJob.com to order guides today!